THE BIBLE: ▶
ENTER HERE

THE BIBLE:
ENTER HERE ➤

*Bringing God's Word to Life
for Today's Teens*

SPENCER C. DEMETROS

THEODOSIA

PRESS

Harvard,
Massachusetts

Theodosia Press
c/o Spencer C. Demetros
4 Cliffside Drive
Harvard, MA 01451
spencer@spencerdemetros.com
https://spencerdemetros.com

Ordering Information:
Quantity sales. Special discounts are available on quantity purchases by corporations, associations, and others. For details, contact the publisher at the address above.

Project Management: Marla Markman, www.MarlaMarkman.com
Editor: Tammy Ditmore, eDitmore Editorial Services, www.editmore.com
Cover design: Tamara Dever, TLC Book Design
Interior design: Marisa Jackson for TLC Book Design

People silhouettes © Depositphotos.com/TAlexey, © Depositphotos.com/dip2000, and © Depositphotos.com/juliarstudio; large arrow banner © Depositphotos.com/a1vector

All Scripture quotations contained in this book are taken from the World English Bible (WEB). It is with sincere appreciation that the author thanks the publishers of the WEB for making its exceptionally accurate, reliable, and readable translation of the Holy Bible available in the public domain. It is a testament to the WEB publishers' loving and selfless commitment to making God's Word readily and openly available throughout the world for evangelism, Bible study, and discipleship.

Publisher's Cataloging-in-Publication Data

Names: Demetros, Spencer C., author.
Title: The Bible : enter here , bringing God's word to life for today's teens / Spencer C. Demetros.
Description: Harvard, MA: Theodosia Press, 2021.
Identifiers: LCCN: 2021908989 | ISBN: 978-1-7371200-0-1 (paperback) | 978-1-7371200-1-8 (eReaders) | 978-1-7371200-2-5 (audio)
Subjects: LCSH Bible--Study and teaching. | Teenagers--Religious life. | Conduct of life. | Christian life. | BISAC YOUNG ADULT NONFICTION / Religion / Biblical Stories & Studies | RELIGION / Biblical Studies / General
Classification: LCC BV4531.3 .D46 2021 | DDC 248.8/3--dc23

Printed in the United States of America

This book is dedicated to my children, Christopher and Coco, God's most precious gift to my beautiful wife, Catherine, and me. For your steadfast refusal to accept anything less than uncompromised clarity, honesty, and relatability during our nightly Bible and prayer time. If not for that, this book never would have been written.

And to Catherine, whose loving, kind, and joyful heart inspires everything good in me.

I HAVE NO GREATER JOY THAN THIS: TO HEAR ABOUT MY CHILDREN WALKING IN TRUTH.

3 JOHN 1:4

TABLE OF
CONTENTS

PART TWO: THE NEW TESTAMENT

175

INTRODUCTION

Every one of us shares the desire to be happy and fulfilled. However, there is one thing that separates you from most others. Because you picked up this book, chances are, you tried the world's recipe for happiness and fulfillment and have come to the realization that it just doesn't work. The world's way—focused on self-interest, pridefulness, pleasure-seeking, and combativeness—leads only to feelings of emptiness, isolation, and despair.

The good news is, in your quest for something better, you were led to the right place. This book is devoted to the one true path to a joyful, meaningful, and eternal life. And that starts and ends with our Lord and Savior, Jesus Christ. Jesus turned the world's formula for happiness and fulfillment on its head, teaching us that, in order to save your life, you have to surrender it—to God. And you no longer can put yourself first, but must serve others, love everyone (including your enemies), and fulfill God's unique plan for your life here on earth.

But how do we apply those words to our daily lives? Well, the Lord has given us a detailed roadmap that leads us to him and ultimately to his Heavenly Kingdom. And that, of course, is the Holy Bible.

The problem is, these days, fewer and fewer people, especially young people, are turning to God's Holy Word. As a result, they are losing the key to God's gift of salvation and eternal life. That's where this book steps in.

WHY THIS BOOK?

The Bible: Enter Here retells the key stories and teachings of the Holy Bible, but in a way that is clear, entertaining, and relevant to the lives of young people. I originally wrote the stories in this book for my own boy-girl twins, Coco and Christopher. When they were little, they loved when my wife, Catherine, and I would read to them from their children's Bibles, with their cartoony pictures, simple language, and selection of only the most colorful Bible stories. But once they hit their preteen years, when we had to start reading from the full Bible, our nightly devotional time went downhill, and fast.

The kids complained that they were bored to tears and felt that much of what we read was unrelatable to their own lives. They also grumbled that, in their view, a lot of the actual Bible text was dry, densely written, and confusing. I pointed out to them that, not only does the Bible unlock the answers to life's most important questions, but it also contains some of the most dramatic and powerful stories ever told. But the truth is, I remembered reading the Bible when I was their age and feeling the same way. In other words, I got their point.

So I started my search for a book that presents the key stories and teachings of the Bible in a way that is enjoyable and relatable for preteens, teenagers, and young adults. Although I expected to find a handful of options to choose from, after scouring both bookstores and the internet, I was shocked to learn that the book I so desperately needed simply didn't exist. So I prayed to God for help.

I felt that the Lord heard my prayers, but was offering an unexpected solution: "You, my dear child, need to tell your kids the key Bible stories and teachings in your own words. But make sure it's entertaining, clear, and relevant to their own lives. Oh yeah, and make it funny." I thought, "Lord, couldn't you just ask me to build an ark in the middle of the desert, or slay a giant with a slingshot? That would be SO much easier!"

WHY ME?

While I saw the value in *someone* taking on this task, my question to God was: "Why me?" Although I've studied the Bible and countless books on Christianity for most of my life, I am not a professional theologian or minister. In fact, I'm as flawed as they come. I mean, I'm a lawyer, for gosh sake! But it soon dawned on me: that's precisely why God was calling *me* to do this.

In my day-job as an attorney, I have to cut through piles of information and boil it down to just the relevant facts. And then I have to communicate logical conclusions based on those facts in a straightforward and convincing way. Also, I've been trained to differentiate between what is true and what is not. While wondering why the Lord was challenging me to perform this assignment, I recognized that I could tap into these skills to present matters of God and faith to a skeptical audience, like my own kids. I knew they would reject any teaching or viewpoint that offends their sense of logic or truth. Apart from all that, my greatest joy in life has always been to tell stories and make people laugh. And my irreverent sense of humor seems to play well with young people.

Feeling that I had some understanding of why the Lord called me to this task, I put pen to paper. When I first read to Coco and Christopher my version of familiar stories like Adam and Eve, Noah's Ark, and Jacob and Esau, I was pleased that the kids clearly enjoyed them and stayed fully engaged. After about a year of writing these stories, I had amassed quite a collection. That's when I began thinking that my writings could be useful to other families with young readers who had matured beyond the age for kid-Bibles. So I made a list of the remaining stories and teachings that I needed to cover, polished up what I had already written, and the rest, as they say, was history.

JUST TO CLARIFY

The Bible: Enter Here is designed to be read and used in several ways. First, young readers can pick it up to read it on their own; this book was written specifically for them. But it can also be used in family devotional time, Bible study groups, or religious school classes. The stories are great for reading aloud, and they are designed to stimulate questions and conversation. You'll find "What Do You Think?" at the end of each chapter. These are questions provided to further inspire conversations and deeper exploration of the biblical stories and topics.

Now, before you embark on what I hope is an enjoyable and meaningful journey through this book, I need to be clear about what this book is, and what it is not. First, on what it is. *The Bible: Enter Here* strives to breathe life into biblical people, including our Lord Jesus Christ, who were not just two-dimensional historical figures. They were real human beings, with real feelings and personalities, who struggled with many of the same challenges we all face. The goal is to help readers appreciate that the Bible's messages are just as relevant to us, in our lives today, as they were when Jesus walked the earth.

In many places in this book, I imagined what a character might have thought or said, and I explored those possible feelings and actions in paraphrases and contemporary vocabulary. In many others, I turned directly to the Bible to reveal the power of God's words. Those direct quotations are marked with book, chapter, and verse.

Finally, a word on what this book is not. It is NOT a substitute for the Holy Bible. Don't shortchange yourself by thinking that if you read this book you will never need to crack open the actual Bible. The Bible citations at the beginning of each chapter are there for a reason; please use them. So enjoy the book, learn from it, and then go back to God's Holy Word and experience first-hand the life-giving treasures contained in the greatest book ever written.

PART ONE:
THE OLD TESTAMENT

Be strong and courageous.
Don't be afraid.
Don't be dismayed, for ...
God is with you wherever you go.

(JOSHUA 1:9)

Chapter 1

IN THE BEGINNING

(GENESIS 1; 2:1–3)

The Bible's account of the creation of the universe began with God's formation of heaven and earth. The earth was covered in darkness, so the Lord spoke and said, "'Let there be light,' and there was light" (Gen. 1:3). God then separated the day from the night, the skies from the waters below, and the waters from dry land. He also called forth living creatures to fill the seas, the skies, and the land and eventually created humans too. God took six days to create the universe and on the seventh day, he rested.

So simple, right? Well, not quite. The fact is, the creation story leaves so many important questions unanswered. Plus, it raises a few of its own. For example:

- If God created the universe, then who created God?
- If nobody created God, then that means he had to always exist. How is that possible? Everything has to have a starting point.

- Why did God even create us? Are we just characters in God's latest video game? Or maybe our entire universe is just one big reality TV show here for God's amusement. Are we humans just the cosmic equivalent of the Kardashians!?
- And how could God be in the room with us right now, watching us, listening to us, and paying attention to everything we're doing while, at the same time, doing that for the other 7.6 billion people on Earth? We know God's a good multitasker but, I mean, come on ...

You've probably wondered about these sorts of things yourself. When my kids would ask me these questions, I never pretended to have all the answers. I told them the truth: that there are certain questions that we'll never have complete answers to, at least in this lifetime. But as long as we believe in an all-powerful God who truly loves us, then we can live with some amount of uncertainty. However, all of this begs the most important question that we all must answer for ourselves: Does God exist?

That is the question that lies "in the beginning" of each of our own spiritual journeys here on earth. And humankind has been struggling with that question since we were shivering in the dark hoping that some smart person would hurry up and discover fire. As for me, my own belief that God is real and has a hand in every part of our lives has been a long time in the making.

When I was a little kid, I believed in God because my parents told me to. But by the time I was eleven or twelve, I started to question everything, including what I had been told about God, Christianity, and what happens to us after we die. It wasn't that I suddenly rejected it all. It's just that the explanations my mom and dad were giving me didn't make much sense to me anymore. I started to wonder more about why we were put here on Earth. And the question of whether God is real became more and more important to me. I felt like I *needed* to know the answer.

So I set out on a quest to determine whether God existed. First, I went straight to the source—you know, the Big Guy upstairs. I got on my knees and asked God to show me a sign to prove to me that he was real. In fact, I begged him. I made clear that I wasn't looking for anything spectacular. The skies didn't need to open up, and the angels didn't need to come cascading down from the clouds while the heavenly choir belted out "How Great Thou Art."

I would have been satisfied with a modest little miracle—just something that couldn't happen without some divine intervention. All I needed was something like a robin perched outside my bedroom window telling me in plain English that God was real and not just a make-believe character developed to get kids to behave. I prayed, "Come on, God, just one little talking bird? Is that really asking too much?"

I upped the ante by offering God a deal: "Please, please, PLEASE just give me a sign that you exist and I promise I'll be the perfect Christian for the rest of my life. I'll honor my father and mother (even when they're being total jerks to me). I won't make wax fingertips with the melted tops of the candles during Good Friday services. And, when I'm serving as altar boy, I promise I won't incinerate any more flies in the priest's incense burner."

I'm not sure what made me think God would choose to reveal himself to little ol' me. I think I believed that if I pleaded often and hard enough, he would see how sincere I was and grant my request, kind of like Linus and the Great Pumpkin. My sincerity would win him over so he would choose my pumpkin patch—or, in this case, my bedroom—to make a brief personal appearance. Unfortunately, that never happened.

When it became obvious that I was not going to be able to order personalized proof from God, I opted for a more tried-and-true approach. I started praying more regularly and making an effort to pay closer attention to what my priest and Sunday school teachers said. I also did something I had never really done before: I cracked open my Bible.

Although I found much of what I read tough to understand, I remember stumbling upon one passage that spoke to me in a big way: "Ask, and it will be given you. Seek, and you will find. Knock, and it will be opened for you" (Matt. 7:7). Well, that seemed pretty clear, right there in black and white. God seemed to be making a promise to anyone who searches for him: just make the effort, reach out, and God will take you by the hand and let you know he's with you.

From that point on, I was even more committed to finding God. And, although I never did get a talking bird in my window, I believe God did reveal himself to me. The signs I received were subtle, but real, and came at different points in my life and in various ways. Sometimes I felt God's presence when I witnessed some extraordinary act of human kindness. In those moments, I felt acutely aware that human beings are biologically wired for self-interest, self-preservation, and survival—just like all other members of the animal kingdom. So, when I saw someone do something that was completely selfless and motivated by nothing but pure love or compassion for another human being, it

served as a sign to me that God exists and someho\
hearts and is at work in our less-than-perfect world.

Sometimes I would witness something that wou.
that previously seemed unremarkable, like the birth c ⌣ baby.
But I viewed it in a completely different light, and could clearly
see God's hand in it. A perfect example is when my children were
born. In that moment, it was crystal clear to me that their creation was nothing short of a miracle. I had long understood the
scientific explanation for how babies are created in a process that
involves fallopian tubes, chromosomes, fertilization, zygotes,
blah, blah, blah. But when I first looked into the eyes of Coco
and Christopher, I could see with laser-sharp clarity that the scientific explanation didn't tell the whole story. The idea that these
conscious beings could be created from a bunch of hydrocarbons
without the intervention of an all-powerful, all-knowing, and loving Creator was simply illogical—it just couldn't happen.

Other times, however, I turned my back on my faith and let my
life go totally off the rails. In those times, when I hit rock bottom
and felt the most empty and without hope, I felt the very real presence of God lifting me up in his arms, taking me out of harm's way,
and setting me back on the path toward a safe and joyful existence.

All that to say, I am a true believer in God. Of course, there still
are moments when I have my doubts; I believe everyone does. But
my doubting moments most often come when I let the distractions of the world divert my attention from the Lord. That's when
I know I need to get back on my knees and knock on the door all
over again. And, sooner or later, the door reopens.

That tells you just a bit about my own faith journey. The information might come in handy as you make your way through this

book, especially if you've been asking your own questions lately. In reading about the real people in the true stories from the Bible, you'll see that everyone, even the Lord's most devoted followers, sometimes struggle with issues of God and faith. But as I learned through my own spiritual quest, those who seek God do find him or, more accurately, finally see that he was there all along.

So if you haven't already done so, you must decide whether you're ready to embark on your own spiritual journey and seek, and ultimately embrace, our Heavenly Father and our savior, Jesus Christ. If you do, the Lord certainly will fulfill his promise and reveal himself to you. He probably won't send a talking bird to perch on your windowsill, but he will make himself known to you in his own time and in his own way. And when he does, it will change your life forever.

It all begins with you: asking, seeking, knocking.

WHAT DO YOU THINK?

- What things in your life support the belief that God indeed exists?
- What ideas of God might cause you to question his existence? Are you able to put those aside and accept that there are just some things we will never be able to understand in our lifetime?
- Why doesn't God just give us each one supernatural sign to prove his existence? Wouldn't that solve everything?
- How do we knock on God's door? What actions can we take that say, "God, let me in"?

Chapter 2

THAT BETTER HAVE BEEN ONE DARN TASTY APPLE!

(GENESIS 2:4–25; 3)

The Bible tells us the very first person who walked the earth was Adam. God created Adam from the dust of the ground and then filled his lungs with divine breath, literally breathing life into him. Adam lived in the Garden of Eden, a beautiful paradise with plenty of great food and not much hard work to do. Adam's only problem? He was lonely. So God put Adam into a deep sleep, took one of his ribs, and used that rib as the building block to create a companion for the man. Adam named her Eve.

Life in the Garden of Eden was free and easy for Adam and Eve. They didn't know about sin, so they ran around naked in their joyful innocence. In fact, there was little they weren't allowed to do. God gave them only one rule that they could NOT break. They were allowed to eat the fruit of any tree in the Garden, but not the fruit of the Tree of Knowledge of Good and Evil (not exactly a catchy name, but it definitely gets the point across). The Bible doesn't say specifically what kind of fruit grew from this tree, but most people today describe the tempting fruit as an apple, so we'll go with that.

Now, if Adam and Eve were anything like me—and apparently they were—after learning that the apple was the ultimate no-no, they started thinking: "Boy, that must be one incredibly delicious apple. I would love just a little taste."

Things got interesting when an annoying talking snake, who probably was one of the Devil's evil minions, came onto the scene. One day, when Eve was alone, the snake sparked up a conversation with her. He told her that eating the apple from the forbidden tree would give her God's wisdom, and she would learn about things like sin and evil. Eve just couldn't resist, so she took a bite of the apple, and convinced Adam to do the same. And that changed the course of humankind forever.

After Eve and Adam ate the apple, their eyes were opened to sin. They immediately felt shame and covered up their naked bodies with fig leaves. When God saw what they had done, he was not happy. He told them they would have to leave the Garden and live the rest of their lives in the world that we all know: full of hard work and its share of pain and sadness.

So is this ultimately a story about produce selection? Of course not. It's primarily a story about our sinful nature and the nasty consequences we face when we give in to temptation.

But there are two other important lessons to be learned from this story. The first has to do with God's reaction when he figured out that Adam and Eve had eaten the apple, breaking the only commandment he had given them. God didn't respond by immediately snuffing them out and going back to the drawing board with a new and improved mother and father of all humanity. Instead, he gave them a slap and sent them out into the cold, cruel world outside of the Garden. That way, they, and all of their descendants, could learn the hard way that the only path to happiness is through obedience to God, so that we can fulfill his plan for each and every one of us. Like our own parents, God loves and forgives us, but sometimes he has to put the hammer down for our own good.

The second lesson comes from considering why Adam and Eve disobeyed that one command. My sense is, Adam and Eve, like us, probably wouldn't have been satisfied living their entire lives as happy-go-lucky children who never learned the whole truth—the good, bad, and ugly—about real life. God created human beings with unlimited curiosity and a free will that leads us to choose wisdom and understanding over blissful ignorance, even if that means getting tossed out of paradise, at least temporarily.

In other words, God must have known that, in the end, Adam and Eve would eat the apple and have to leave the Garden. But he had bigger plans for them and for the rest of humanity that require a short stint here in our imperfect world. That is the only way for us to experience all of the joys, the sorrows, the failures, and the triumphs that come with being fully human.

WHAT DO YOU THINK?

- If you were Adam or Eve, and you knew ahead of time what the effects of eating the apple would be, would you have eaten it anyway?
- In your own life, how have you eaten of God's forbidden fruit? What motivated you to do so? Did you regret it? Why or why not?

Chapter 3

NOTE TO SELF: NEXT TIME, DON'T HOLD BACK ON THE PRIZED ARTICHOKES

(GENESIS 4:1–16)

Not long after Adam and Eve got tossed out of the Garden of Eden, they learned God wasn't kidding about how tough life would be in the real world. That's because their two oldest sons, Cain and Abel, became the main characters in the world's very first tale of jealousy, revenge, and murder!

Cain, the older of the two boys, was a farmer. Younger brother Abel was a shepherd. One day, the brothers decided to offer a sacrifice to God. That's what people did back then, offer something nice to God and hope to stay in his good graces. Cain gave a portion of his harvest, and Abel sacrificed the best sheep from his flock.

As it turns out, God was pleased with Abel's offering. Cain's? Not so much. The Bible doesn't tell us exactly why God wasn't satisfied with the fruits and veggies Cain offered up. Maybe he kept the juiciest peaches and sweetest mangoes for himself and offered God nothing but brussels sprouts and spinach. Who knows? In any case, God let Cain know that he wasn't the least bit wowed by what Cain had brought him.

Sometime later, God approached Cain, who was moping around and feeling sorry for himself, still angry because God had dissed his sacrifice. God told Cain to knock it off with the long face and move on. When you sin, God said, you will suffer the consequences, but when you work to please me, like your brother Abel did, you will reap the rewards.

Cain could have taken God's constructive criticism to heart and tried harder the next time. But he didn't. He just kept sulking, growing more and more resentful. And that's when things got really ugly.

One day, while the brothers were out in the fields, Cain did the unthinkable: he killed Abel. Not long after, God showed up and asked Cain where he might find his brother. Cain got defensive, saying something to the effect of: "How would I know? Maybe he was eaten by one of those oh-so-fabulous sheep of his."

Of course, God knew exactly what had happened. "What have you done?" God asked Cain. "The voice of your brother's blood cries to me from the ground" (Gen. 4:10). God could not let Cain get away with literal murder, so he punished him by sending him away. The Lord forced him to leave his family and his farm and become a wanderer for the rest of his life. "You will be a fugitive and a wanderer in the earth," God said (Gen. 4:12).

A little bit of good news does come out of this very sad story. God gave Adam and Eve more children and, as far as we know, none of them became murderers or perpetrators of other heinous acts of violence.

The story of Cain and Abel reveals the destructive power of anger and jealousy. Cain became so furious and so jealous when he watched God praise Abel that he actually killed his little brother. In the process, he not only ended the life of his own flesh and blood, but he also ruined his own life. Ironically, the whole thing started with Cain simply wanting to please God.

Thankfully, the Bible shows us that God forgave Cain even while holding him accountable for his sin. He allowed Cain to live out the rest of his life, albeit not in his chosen profession as a farmer nor with his family. The Lord even protected Cain from anyone who might want to kill him to avenge Abel's death (Gen. 4:15).

If God will forgive a man who killed his brother, it seems pretty clear that there isn't much we can do that we can't be forgiven for, if we repent of those sins. The Lord's grace is infinite and, even in the face of the worst sins imaginable, God always loves his children.

WHAT DO YOU THINK?

- Why was God so hard on Cain about his offering? Does that seem unfair?
- What do you think was going on inside Cain's head that caused him to kill his own brother?
- Can you think of any sin that might be unforgivable?

Chapter 4

SOMEONE HELP! THE IGUANAS JUST JUMPED OVERBOARD!

(GENESIS 6–8; 9:1–17)

The next time you're complaining about something you're called to do for your Christian faith, just think about poor Noah and his ark. God asked him to build a giant boat, miles from any body of water, in one of the driest climates in the world. And this boat had to accommodate a male and female of every type of animal on earth—from the biggest elephants, to the slimiest maggots, to the most annoying laughing hyenas.

When his buddies asked him why he was doing all of this, Noah could only say: "Because God told me a flood is coming that's going to kill everyone and everything on earth, including you." We can safely assume Noah's name was scratched off the invitation list for the neighborhood cookout after that conversation.

Although everyone thought Noah had become nuttier than a fruitcake, he turned out to be right. Apparently, God wasn't just the creator of the universe and everything in it. He also was a darn good weather forecaster. After Noah got his ark built and gathered his family and all those animals inside, it started raining. And it kept raining, just like God had predicted.

It rained for forty days and forty nights, flooding the earth and killing everything and everyone except for those packed inside the ark. Eventually, the waters receded, and Noah, his family, and the animals emerged from the ark and began repopulating the earth.

Noah's story shows us how God can call one man to take actions that might appear irrational in order to save himself and his family. When he was following God's orders and building a mammoth boat, the rest of the world thought Noah was insane. But then, Noah had always seemed a little bit odd even before he started building the ark. He didn't join his neighbors' drunken parties or depraved sexual encounters. He also wasn't bent on lying, cheating, and picking fights with anyone who crossed him, even though that is how everyone around him behaved. That's why Noah found favor with God. He had already proved that he could go against the grain of the wicked culture all around him.

Our culture seems remarkably like the one that Noah lived in. We are surrounded by sin. If you have any doubt, just watch an hour of reality TV, look at the trending videos on YouTube, or visit the popular social media sites. You will see that crude language, aggression toward others, narcissism, and an unhealthy obsession with sex are not only tolerated, but glorified. Sadly, our "entertainment" reflects not only what is going on in the world around us, but also what is in our own hearts.

Thankfully, there's hope for those of us who are willing to stand firm in the face of sin and immorality, just like Noah did.

We can choose a path that will lead to eternal happiness—both in this world and the next. We just need to take that bold step and build our own ark so we can remove ourselves from the destructive influences that surround us 24/7.

I'm not suggesting that you should construct a giant boat to escape to or hide from the world on top of a mountain or under your bed covers. I'm just encouraging you to unplug and give yourself a break from the junk on TV and your phones. And if you're hanging with a crowd that is dragging you down the rathole of sin, you might need to find a new crowd. Remove the destructive influences from your life and devote yourself to following our Lord and Savior Jesus Christ. Soon, you'll feel the heavy burden of sin being lifted from your shoulders.

Of course, your problems won't instantly go away, and your life won't always be easy. But answering God's call to set yourself apart from the sinful excesses of our culture will open your eyes to your potential to achieve greatness in this world. And walking with God will allow you to experience the joy, the peace, and the hope that he promises to all of his devoted children.

When Noah and his family were finally able to leave the ark and set themselves up on dry land again, God promised them he would never again use a flood to wipe out human life, and he marked his covenant with a rainbow. Whenever we see a rainbow in the sky, we recognize it as a symbol of God's promise to Noah (Gen. 9:8–17). And we are reassured that our Good Lord *does* keep his promises.

WHAT DO YOU THINK?

- Have you ever seen someone do something in the name of God that seemed irrational?
- If you think God might be calling you to do something, how can you know whether it's really God and not just your mind playing tricks on you?
- Do you sometimes feel that the sinful and destructive influences of our current popular culture are bringing you down and making you unhappy? Have you considered unplugging from those influences and focusing on activities that will bring you closer to God?
- Would making that change bring you more or less joy and peace in your life?

Chapter 5

DOES ANYONE KNOW HOW TO SAY "NAIL GUN" IN CHALDEAN?

(GENESIS 11:1–9)

After Noah's family began to repopulate the earth, the generations that followed stuck together and settled on a plain called Shinar. There, they developed a city that could comfortably house all of their people and act as a home-base to keep everyone together like one big, happy family. They liked the place so much that they decided to build a huge tower in the middle of the city—basically the ancient world's equivalent of a skyscraper.

God saw what they were doing, and he was not pleased. First, he wasn't happy that the people had developed this nesting instinct because he wanted people to spread throughout the world, not stay hunkered down in one spot, like a colony of ants. And building a tower that reached up into the heavens? God took that as a challenge to his supreme authority over the earth.

So God threw a monkey wrench into the project with one little move: he rewired the people's brains so that they no longer shared one common language. It instantly became like a meeting of the United Nations—everyone speaking in different tongues—but without the translators. One guy would ask for a hammer in Arabic, and the next guy, who had suddenly started speaking Sumerian, would hand him a trowel.

God's little prank on the people of Shinar worked perfectly. The construction project came to a grinding halt. The people abandoned their tower, split up, and ventured forth into the world. The unfinished tower became known as the Tower of Babel because that is where God "confused the language of all the earth" (Gen. 11:9).

The tale of the Tower of Babel reveals one of the Lord's most fundamental truths: he did not intend for humanity to be all one and the same. The fact that we all are members of different races, from different ethnic backgrounds, and are unique in our talents, our physical appearances, and our personalities is very much a deliberate part of God's plan for humankind. After Noah's descendants made some headway in populating the earth, God intervened to scatter the world's people, all of whom were congregating around the plain of Shinar, and diversify them.

Suddenly dividing people by giving them different languages forced them to separate and disperse into every direction, setting into motion the development of a planet that is racially, ethnically, and culturally diverse. And the Lord derailed the efforts of the people of Shinar to build a tower that reached into the heavens, making clear that no one group of people should reign supreme. That honor goes to God and God alone.

As Christians, we're called upon to overcome the sinful and destructive forces that can cause us to fear, mistrust, or even hate people, just because they're different from us. The Lord instructs us to love everyone, so we should celebrate each other's differences, recognizing those differences as an essential and glorious part of God's grand design for humanity.

WHAT DO YOU THINK?

- What are some current examples of people trying to build their own Tower of Babel? In other words, what do people do to elevate their own power and glory instead of God's?
- Do you think the Lord disapproves of all truly great achievements of humankind? Which ones do you think he approves? Which ones might be more like the Tower of Babel in his eyes?
- How would the world be a different place if everyone spoke the same language? What would our world be like if we all shared one cultural or ethnic background?
- Why do you think God created humans with different skin colors and hair textures and facial features?

Chapter 6

SHE LOOKS NOTHING LIKE HIM! (I'LL BETCHA THEY WERE ADOPTED)

(GENESIS 12)

After the descendants of Noah received their lesson on diversity from the whole Tower of Babel debacle, the people disbanded and spread throughout the world. One of these world-travelers, Abram, was very much favored by God. And, unbeknownst to Abram at the time, he would someday take his place as the founding forebearer of the Jewish people.

Abram was married to a woman named Sarai, who was extremely beautiful. God instructed Abram to leave his father's house with Sarai and his nephew, Lot, "and go to the land that I will show you" (Gen. 12:1). During one stop in the land of Canaan, God told Abram to gaze out onto the land. The Lord then promised that this entire region, as far as Abram's eyes could see, would belong to Abram's future descendants.

But it wasn't long before a horrible famine struck that region, so Abram temporarily moved his crew to Egypt, where he hoped there would be at least enough food to survive. And here is where the story gets a bit weird. Because Sarai was quite the looker, Abram worried that the Egyptian men would see her and want to marry her. In fact, Sarai was such a good prospect, Abram reasoned, that men might be willing to remove him from the equation—in other words, kill him—just to get to her.

Whether this actually would have happened or was just a product of Abram's paranoia, we'll never know for sure. But Abram wasn't taking any chances. So, he told the Egyptians that Sarai was his sister. Sure enough, the Egyptian Pharaoh saw Sarai and was smitten, so he brought her into his palace as one of his wives. Believing Abram was Sarai's brother, the Pharaoh gave Abram livestock, camels, servants, and plenty of riches to please Abram and keep Sarai happy.

But God was not happy that Pharaoh had taken another man's wife, so the Lord sent some nasty plagues to the Pharaoh's house to punish him and his family. Somehow, Pharaoh figured out that Sarai was really Abram's wife, and that was the reason he was being tormented with the plagues. The Egyptian ruler immediately fixed the situation. He called Abram on the carpet for lying to him. Pharaoh then sent Abram, Sarai, and Lot out of Egypt with all of their livestock and wealth, and hoped that they would never darken his door again.

So, is God trying to tell us that acting cowardly and passing your wife off as your sister will ultimately get you lots of fancy riches? Well, no. But he is showing us that even the people whom God most loved and favored were incredibly flawed human beings. You could argue that Abram was just trying to feed his family, but there is just no way to believe that Abram acted honorably in this situation.

Fortunately, this isn't the only story we have about Abram. And when you read Abram's whole story, you will see that, for most of his life, Abram proved to be a faithful man of God who deserves his prominent place in the history of God's people.

As you make your way through your journey here on earth, remember that the qualities you have at the beginning of your trip are not what matters the most. Every one of us is imperfect, after all. What ultimately matters is what you do with your life. And the only path to reaching your highest potential is through keeping the Lord close, staying obedient to him, and growing as a Christian by seeking his guidance as you face life's many challenges.

WHAT DO YOU THINK?

- Why do you think Abram did not trust God to protect him and Sarai in Egypt? In other words, why did Abram feel he needed to lie about Sarai?
- Do you think it was unfair for God to punish Pharaoh when Pharaoh didn't know Sarai was really Abram's wife? Can you think of any justification for God's actions?
- Abram, who God later named "Abraham," is one of the most revered figures in the Jewish faith and culture. Why would God include this story about Abram's less-than-honorable behavior in the Bible?

Chapter 7

LIFELONG EMPTY NESTERS GET A BABY BIRDIE

(GENESIS 13; 15:1–6; 17; 18:1–15)

Abram, Sarai, and Lot made their way out of Egypt with their livestock, gold, silver, and other valuables. Over time, Abram's and Lot's herds became so big that their workers were getting in each other's way and butting heads more and more. The two men therefore decided to part ways. Lot went east and claimed the fertile land of the Plain of Jordan, and Abram settled in Canaan, the land that God had pledged to him, the so-called "Promised Land."

Life in Canaan was good for Abram and Sarai except for one thing: they were in their old age and Sarai had no children. Abram did have a son, Ishmael, who had been born to Sarai's servant, Hagar. But Abram and Sarai had no child of their own. However, God had a plan for them, which included a little bundle of joy named Isaac. The conversation leading up to this joyous event probably went something like this:

Abram: Honey, I have something I need to talk to you about.

Sarai: Don't tell me, you found a great deal on a new camel. Look, Abram, I told you a hundred times, NO MORE CAMELS until we finish furnishing the tent. I'm embarrassed to have people over. We've had this junk since the year we left Egypt.

Abram: No, it's not about a camel—although I did find one for cheap that is so strong, it could carry a mountain across the Sinai Desert. But we can talk about that later. After I tell you my *incredible* news. Are you ready?

Sarai: Do I have a choice?

Abram: We're going to be parents!

Sarai: Parents? What are you talking about?

Abram: Well, I was talking to God, and he told me that you are going to bear me a son.

Sarai: Abram, have you been dipping into the ceremonial wine again? How could I bear you a son? I'm an old lady. I can barely reach down to tie my own sandals. And, while we're on the subject, you are ninety-nine years old! How could we possibly have a baby? I think that ship sailed a long time ago.

Abram: I know it sounds crazy, but God said we'll have more descendants than there are stars in the sky.

Sarai: Oh really? Did God tell you anything else, like when I'm going to get my new furniture? It would be nice if, when I'm pregnant, my ninety-year-old buttocks won't get sore from sitting on that stone sofa in the family room.

Abram: Honey, be serious. This is our chance to finally have our own baby.

Sarai: Okay, I'm sorry. This just doesn't seem possible. Actually, I have a confession to make. The other day, when you were talking to those three men—the ones you said were sent by God—I overheard them saying something about me having a baby. It made me laugh out loud! Just think—me, a new mother at such an old age. But now you're telling me you think this is really going to happen?

Abram: Yes, I know it will; God told me so directly. He also said something that was a bit weird.

Sarai: Something weirder than the two of us old fossils having a baby?

Abram: Well, he said that, starting now, I and every single one of our male descendants will have to be circumcised as a symbol that we accept the Lord's covenant that he will forever be the God of our people.

Sarai: Circumcise? You mean, you have to take that little flap of skin—

Abram: Yep!

Sarai: The skin around the top of your—

Abram: Yep!

Sarai: And cut it off?!

Abram: You got it!

Sarai: Ahh! I think I'm going to faint!

Abram: Relax, honey. I'll take care of that little procedure.

Sarai: You got that right. Did God say anything else?

Abram: Just one more thing. He changed our names.

Sarai: Well, now we're talking! I always wanted a name that's a bit more catchy than Sarai. Did the Lord give me a pretty name? Something like Jasmine, or Gabriella, or Hemaroya?

Abram: Hemaroya? What kind of name is that?

Sarai: I made it up. Isn't it pretty? Hema means blood, and roya stands for royalty. I like to think that I have the blood of true royalty, like a queen. Do you like it?

Abram: I don't know, it sounds too much like hemorrhoid. Don't you think?

Sarai: No, I don't "*think*"! But hemorrhoid might as well be my name if I have to sit on that hard sofa much longer. So tell me, what is my new name?

Abram: It's Sarah.

Sarah: Sarah? That's it? Sarah? That's not a new name. He just dropped the "i" and added an "h." He's the creator of the entire universe—and that's the best he could come up with?

Abram: The name Sarah means princess.

Sarah: Princess? Really? Well, I do have to say, Sarah does have a nice ring to it. It kind of goes with my whole "blood of royalty" theme, don't you think?

Abram: Yes, dear. And my new name is Abraham.

Sarah: Abraham?! He just added a syllable? He just stuck "ham" at the end of your name? Our people don't even eat ham!

Abraham: Sweetie, Abraham means "father of many."

Sarah: Look, "father of many," I'm sorry for being so salty. It's just that this is all so overwhelming. I don't know if I'm up for this.

Abraham: But having a baby is something you've always wanted; and you deserve this. I had asked God to give us a child for so long, I figured he wasn't answering my prayers because I'm just not a good person.

Sarah: Now why would you say that? That's not true.

Abraham: Yes it is. I've done some pretty horrible things in my life.

Sarah: Like what?

Abraham: Well, I've never quite forgiven myself for what I did in Egypt. You know, passing you off as my sister just to save my own neck. So, part of me wonders why God is giving us this incredible blessing when I've done some things that I'm so ashamed of.

Sarah: Maybe God looks past your flaws and sees what I do: a kind and gentle soul with a pure heart. Can I tell you something, Abram—sorry, I mean, Abraham?

Abraham: What is it?

Sarah: You're a good man. And I love you very much.

Abraham: I love you too, Sarah. And I think you're going to be a wonderful mother.

And so it began …

WHAT DO YOU THINK?

- Why do you think God waited until Abram and Sarai were very old before blessing them with their own baby boy?
- Have you ever had to wait for God to answer one of your prayers? Afterward, were you able to see some reason why God had a different timetable than you did?
- The Lord often changed the names of people dear to him. Why do you think he changed Abram and Sarai to Abraham and Sarah?

Chapter 8

WHY IS MOM BEING SO SALTY?

(GENESIS 18:16–33; 19:1–29)

Not long after God told Abraham that he and Sarah would soon become parents, he paid Abraham another visit. This time, the news wasn't so happy. The Lord told Abraham that he was planning on destroying the nearby cities of Sodom and Gomorrah. His reason? The people who lived there had become so sinful and depraved that they needed to be wiped off the face of the earth.

Abraham was disturbed by this news, and not just because he knew a lot of people would die. He was particularly worried about his nephew, Lot, who lived in Sodom with his wife and daughters. Abraham probed God about whether *everyone* in those cities would have to die. He kept bargaining with God about how many good people would have to be found to keep God from destroying the cities. Eventually, God assured Abraham that he would spare the cities if he could find ten righteous people living in Sodom or Gomorrah.

So God sent a couple of angels, in the form of regular men,

to Sodom to do some investigating. The angels met up with Lot, who invited them to his house for dinner and to spend the night. While the two visitors were inside Lot's home, the men of Sodom surrounded Lot's house and demanded that he bring out the visitors. It was clear to Lot that this crowd intended to cause serious harm to his guests, and Lot pleaded with them to leave the men alone. But the violent mob refused to leave and started to attack Lot, so the angels caused the men of Sodom to go instantly blind. Unable to see, they were forced to abandon their wicked plan.

This horrific confrontation was all that the angels needed to confirm that Sodom and Gomorrah were indeed rotting stink-holes of sin and corruption and worthy of God's wrath. So they told Lot that he and his family needed to leave the city right away because God was going to destroy both Sodom and Gomorrah. The next morning, Lot was taking his sweet time getting ready to leave, so the angels grabbed hold of Lot, his wife, and their two daughters and dragged them out of the city.

"Escape for your life!" the angels told the family. "Don't look behind you!" (Gen. 19:17). As soon as Lot and his family had made it to safety, the Lord poured down sulfur and fire on Sodom and Gomorrah, and everyone and everything that lived there perished. The family was saved from the fiery destruction. But Lot's wife disobeyed the angels' command. She turned and looked back at Sodom and Gomorrah and "she became a pillar of salt" (Gen. 19:26).

It's hard to read this Bible story without thinking, "Really, God, I know Lot's wife peeked over her shoulder and all, but turning her into a pillar of salt? Isn't that just a bit extreme?"

But, in fairness to God, when you put the "pillar of salt" thing in context, it might not seem so crazy.

Let's start with the cities in question, Sodom and Gomorrah. The fact is, every city has its share of temptations, crime, and sin, but God doesn't typically address the problem by wiping out every sign of life that exists there. So Sodom and Gomorrah had to be a special case. In fact, God had promised Abraham that he would spare the cities if there were even ten righteous people living there. Apparently, there were not. These cities were so infected with evil that thousands of years later, their very names remain synonymous with sin and corruption.

So, what about Lot's wife? The Bible's reference to her "looking back" has to mean she did more than just take a little peek to satisfy her curiosity. Who wouldn't look back at their hometown if they knew it was being pelted with sulfur and fire? And why would the angels try to stop that behavior?

It seems likely that the angels' command to "not look back" must take on a different meaning, a deeper purpose. The angels had to be saying something like: "After you've escaped from Sodom, there's no looking back. You better not have any second thoughts about leaving that place behind you, completely and forever. If you think you'll be allowed to carry the contagious germ of evil that pervaded Sodom and Gomorrah to the next place you go, you're sadly mistaken. You need to completely disavow that place and everything it represents or else you won't make it out alive."

As it turns out, Lot's wife couldn't sever her ties with Sodom, and God knew that she had left at least a part of her heart in that wicked place. She wasn't able to move on. In other words, she "looked back."

Sin is a funny thing. We all know that it puts a wedge between us and God and, in the long run, brings nothing but misery. Still, it can be difficult to resist and even harder to stop if you ever give in. A dark force is undoubtedly alive and well in our world. Whether you want to label that force "the Devil," "the Enemy," or just "the force of evil," it is real. And it makes sin attractive and sometimes even fun—until it turns your life upside down. Which is what sin will do to you, sooner or later.

When you finally decide you're going to get out of town and leave your sinful life behind once and for all, be aware that your old bad behaviors will come beckoning, reminding you of the good times, downplaying the destruction and chaos. And if you give in to the temptation and start looking back fondly on the "good old days" when sin ruled your life, you will become mired in a state of spiritual paralysis—a pillar of salt, unable to enter that joyful place of God's brilliant light.

The Bible doesn't pull any punches. It says quite clearly that the wages of sin is death. Not just physical death, but spiritual death as well. Lot's wife provides a very visible example of what happens to someone who chooses to nourish a spirit of evil and corruption. Thankfully, the Bible also gives us hope: "For the wages of sin is death, but the free gift of God is eternal life in Christ Jesus our Lord" (Rom. 6:23).

In other words, we do have a choice. We can buy into the world's biggest lie: that we can be happy and fulfilled even when we disobey our Creator and live separate from him. Or, we can leave our old lives behind and move on, completely and without regret, by fixing our eyes on Jesus and following him. Only then can we be transported into a new place, a place where the heavy burden of sin will be removed from our backs and where we will receive the gift of eternal life, a life that is joyful, meaningful, and truly worth living.

WHAT DO YOU THINK?

- In today's world, why doesn't God just wipe away places where sin and corruption are rampant, as he did with Sodom and Gomorrah?
- Have you ever decided to leave behind you a particular sin but later looked back on your old ways with some degree of longing? Did you go back to the behavior or were you able to resist the temptation to revert to your old ways?
- Do you think there is a difference between struggling with sin inside yourself and struggling with sin that is tied to a place or particular group of people? If so, do you think this difference might influence how you try to overcome the sin in question?

Chapter 9

BIRTH RIGHT, SHMIRTH RIGHT

(GENESIS 25:19–34; 27; 28:1–9)

As God foretold (see chapter 7), Abraham and Sarah did have a son, and they named him Isaac, which means "laughter." (Any idea where that name could have come from?) Eventually, Isaac grew up and married a woman named Rebekah. Together they had twin sons, Jacob and Esau.

Esau was the more manly of the two brothers. He was bigger and stronger than Jacob, liked to hunt, and was really hairy. Jacob was more of a homebody, the type of kid who liked to help his mother around the house instead of going out hunting. In other words, he was the wimpy brother. His idea of a good time was probably organizing his sandal closet or polishing his collection of exotic desert arachnids. And the Bible tells us that Jacob was his mother's favorite.

One day, Esau came in from the great outdoors, probably after doing something manly, like building a tiger trap or wrestling a wild boar. He caught a whiff of something delicious coming out of the kitchen and saw his Domestic Diva brother,

Jacob, stirring a beautiful pot of stew. Esau was *so* hungry, and that stew smelled *so* good.

Jacob saw how desperate Esau was for a bowl of the stew. So he said: "Hey Bro—have I got a deal for you. A giant bowl of this thick and meaty stew, that is just *oozing* with flavor, can be yours for one low price. All you have to do is hand over your birthright."

You're probably wondering, "What's a birthright?" Well, in Jewish tradition, Esau, the firstborn male in the family, had a right to succeed his dad and receive a majority of his father's inheritance. In other words, he was born first, so he had a right to most of the money. This inheritance typically included a father's ceremonial "blessing," which people believed would give the firstborn a huge advantage in life, things like a powerful position in Jewish society. Or a huge family with lots of children (which, in the days before college tuition went through the roof, was considered a good thing).

Jacob knew that Esau's birthright would be more valuable than a winning lottery ticket. So he probably figured getting Esau to agree to his proposed deal was a longshot. But Esau fell for it. Letting his stomach do the thinking, Esau agreed to Jacob's terms and wolfed down what turned out to be an extremely costly meal.

Some time later, Rebekah approached Jacob to hatch a scheme to solidify Jacob's questionably earned entitlement to Esau's paternal blessing. She wanted to help Jacob pull the old switcheroo on Isaac, who couldn't see so well any more, and trick Isaac into blessing the wimpy twin with the silky-smooth skin instead of the macho, hairy twin.

Rebekah had been listening when Isaac sent Esau out to hunt down the perfect piece of wild game so that Esau could make the perfect pre-blessing meal. So Rebekah hurried to give Jacob the makeover of the century to fool his nearly blind father. She outfitted Jacob with Esau's clothes straight off the laundry pile—so Jacob would have Esau-stink all over him. Then she glued goat skin onto Jacob's exposed skin so Isaac would believe he was feeling Esau's furry hands and neck.

Long story short, the con game worked. Isaac thought he was blessing Esau, but instead he blessed Jacob, promising him wealth, power, and prominence in the future legacy of the Jewish people. Needless to say, when Esau came home and learned what had happened, he was furious and vowed to kill his sneaky little brother. And, true to his wimpy nature, Jacob ran away, at least until Esau cooled down.

When I first read this passage, I scratched my head, wondering what positive lesson could be learned from this Bible story. All I saw was: "Yep, liars and cheats do get ahead in this world and even get entire nations named after them." (Did I mention that God later changed Jacob's name to Israel?) But the longer I studied it, the more I realized there is more going on here than "little mama's boy steals blessing from lunkhead brother." The fact is, Rebekah understood that her older son was undisciplined, self-indulgent, and unrestrained. She knew he was so impulsive that he would literally sell his entire birthright for a single bowl of stew.

Rebekah knew her boys well enough to understand that Jacob had the temperament, determination, and other qualities he would need to become the leader of the Jewish people and earn his place in their proud history. In fact, when Rebekah was pregnant with the boys, God had spoken to her and foretold that the younger twin ultimately would win out over the older. The Lord told her, "Two nations are in your womb. Two peoples will be separated from your body. The one people will be stronger than the other people. The elder will serve the younger" (Gen. 25:23). In this way, God informed Rebekah that his plan was for Jacob, not Esau, to receive Isaac's blessing and become heir to God's covenant to make Abraham's descendants into a great nation.

There's a saying: "If you want to make an omelet, you have to break a few eggs." In this case, what needed to be broken was the rule that would have made Esau, solely by virtue of his birth order, one of the forefathers of the Jewish nation. While Rebekah was pregnant with the twins, God informed her of his plan for the two boys. So she did what she felt she had to do.

WHAT DO YOU THINK?

- Esau struggled with delaying physical gratification, even when he knew he would lose some huge future benefit. Do you struggle with that too? What are steps you can take to counteract your impatience?
- Does this story teach that the "ends justify the means"? In other words, if the outcome is good and favorable in the eyes of God, is it then okay to break some rules to achieve the desired result?
- What "rules" were Rebekah and Jacob violating? How important are those rules to the Lord?

Chapter 10

JACOB GETS HIS MOJO ON

(GENESIS 32:22–32)

Have you ever gotten really mad at God? Have you ever blamed the Lord for whatever was making you so unhappy and then unloaded on him? If the answer is "yes," you've probably wondered how God reacted to your anger. "Is the Lord glad I was upfront with him? Or is he furious with me for being so confrontational? Is he going to get back at me? Am I going to hell?!"

To get an idea about how God might react to our anger, let's take a look at what happened when Jacob called out the Lord and wound up in an all-night wrestling match with him. We last saw Jacob running away from Esau, who was ready to kill his brother for tricking a blessing out of their father. Jacob wound up traveling to Haran, where he was taken in by his mother's brother, married a couple of sisters, had a bunch of kids, and got pretty rich—back when riches were counted in sheep and cows. After a couple of decades, he decided to head home, back to Canaan, hoping he had given Esau enough time to cool down from his rage about the birthright and blessing.

One night during this return trip, Jacob sent his family ahead to settle in while he set up camp alone, along the banks of a shallow river called Jabbok. Jacob was then approached by a "man," or at least that's what he's called when he makes his first appearance in this story in Genesis. Later in the story, we find out this man is actually God himself. We don't know exactly what Jacob's gripe with the Lord was on that particular evening, but we do know he got into a long, nasty wrestling match with him.

Although Jacob had been the "wimpy" brother earlier in his life, he apparently was a pretty scrappy fighter by this point. He wrestled God until daybreak, and the Bible tells us that God was not getting the best of Jacob. Even when God poked Jacob's hip socket and whacked a tendon out of place, Jacob kept on fighting.

At one point, Jacob had "the man" in a death-grip. Jacob said he wouldn't let go until God gave him a blessing. Instead of bringing a lightning bolt down on Jacob's head, or a swarm of tarantulas, God did bless Jacob and the fight was over. And the Lord gave Jacob a new name. "Your name will no longer be called Jacob, but Israel; for you have fought with God and with men, and have prevailed" (Gen. 32:28). Jacob knew something pretty special had happened. "I have seen God face to face, and my life is preserved" (Gen. 32:30). Then the sun rose and Jacob limped away.

When you read this story, you can't help but see that you don't have to be perfect to get God's blessing. In fact, sometimes God seems to favor the biggest troublemakers. Jacob, after all, traded a bowl of stew for his brother's birthright and impersonated his furry sibling to trick his poor, blind father. And here he is picking a fight with God, wrestling him to the ground, and demanding a blessing.

The Bible is filled with stories like Jacob's—people who had more than their share of character flaws but still get attention, affection, and blessings from God. I guess that means there's hope for all of us.

In this account of the nightlong wrestling match, we also learn that God not only forgives us when we confront him, but he actually welcomes the confrontation. Let's face it, life can get pretty hard at times. We all have those moments when we're feeling so frustrated and angry that we just want to climb up a mountain and scream: "Okay, God, enough! If you love us, why do you have to bring so much pain into this world? Helloooo? Anybody out there? For once, will you please just answer me?!"

That's usually how my own tirades with the Lord play out. They come when this world has beaten me up, sucked the life out of me, and left me ready to throw in the towel. But whenever I open up to God and honestly tell him about my frustrations and anger, he does answer. Of course, he answers in his own way and in his own time, but he always gives me what I need to carry on.

In his relationship with Jacob, God demonstrates that he is fine with us venting our frustration, our anger, or our disappointment with him, the world he created, or our very lives. He can absorb our disappointments, our questions, our wrestling matches of faith—just as long as we are willing to stay engaged with him. He would much rather listen to your angry questions than deal with your silence. Because there is no way for God to respond when you ignore him or turn your back on him entirely.

So, keep your prayers real and don't hold back your feelings. Like Jacob, sometimes we'll limp away from a battle with God, a bit battered and bruised. But that's okay. Our rewards will out-weigh the costs. The Bible tells us Jacob limped away from his battle with God because of the poke to his hip. But it also tells us that God rewarded Jacob for his dogged persistence. He not only blessed Jacob, but he also bestowed upon him the name "Israel," which became the name of the Jewish nation, the name that continues to this day. A great blessing, indeed.

WHAT DO YOU THINK?

- Have you ever fought with God? Have you ever let God know that you were really furious with him? How did God respond?
- Do you think there is a line you cannot cross when you "fight" with God?

Chapter 11

NOW LET ME TELL YOU ABOUT MY DREAM; IT INVOLVES YOU IN A DEEP DARK HOLE IN THE GROUND!

(GENESIS 37; 39–40; 41:1–57)

I've always been annoyed when people want to tell me their dreams, especially when they just can't resist giving every last boring detail. And they recount it with such pride, like they just wrote the latest Harry Potter sequel.

I try to be polite. I might say something like: "Wow! You escaped the zombie apocalypse by hyperspacing to Mars, where you were attacked by iguana-headed aliens? That is so cool!" But I'm really thinking, "That is the stupidest dream I've ever heard." And then I find myself sympathizing with Joseph's brothers. Because Joseph was one of history's most annoying dream-tellers.

Joseph was one of the twelve sons of Jacob, who had been living a relatively peaceful life with his family in Canaan, the land God had promised to Jacob's grandfather, Abraham. Joseph was the eleventh son but the first in Jacob's heart, which he demonstrated by giving Joseph a beautiful, multicolored coat.

One night, Joseph had a dream that he couldn't resist describing to his brothers. In the dream, they had all been working in the fields, tying up bundles of wheat, when his brothers' bundles suddenly started bowing down to his own bundle. A little later, Joseph had another dream he couldn't wait to share: the sun, the moon, and eleven stars had bowed down to him, as though he were the master and they were his servants. That dream even annoyed his father.

His brothers could hardly stand to watch Joseph strut around like a peacock in his multicolored coat, boasting about his dreams of grandeur. He just set their teeth on edge. So when Jacob sent Joseph out to visit his brothers in the fields where they were watching sheep, the brothers decided this was their chance to get rid of that annoying pest.

They hatched a plot to kill Joseph and blame it on a wild animal. But Reuben, the oldest of the twelve sons, knew murder was a bit harsh, even in the face of the really obnoxious dreams. So he convinced his brothers to throw Joseph into a dry well, thinking he would go back and rescue his little brother later.

But while Reuben was away, the other brothers found a way to get rid of Joseph and pick up some pocket change at the same time. They sold him to some traveling merchants, who loaded Joseph onto one of their camels and carried him off to Egypt. To cover up their crime, the brothers dipped Joseph's beautiful coat in goat's blood and took it back to their father. Jacob took one look at that coat and began wailing, convinced that his favorite son had been eaten by a wild animal.

Jacob sobbed and expressed his profound sorrow, something to the effect of: "I'll never forgive myself. I was the one who sent

Joseph out into the fields. It's my fault he's dead. I'm going to mourn for my son for the rest of my life."

When the merchants got to Egypt, they sold Joseph to a guy named Potiphar, who was in charge of the palace guard for the Egyptian Pharaoh. Joseph worked really hard and Potiphar liked him a lot. But Potiphar's wife liked Joseph even more, which turned into a bad scene, complete with lies that unjustly landed Joseph in prison.

Now prison was no fun. But Joseph eventually worked his way out because he could interpret other people's dreams. God had given him the gift of dream interpretation. Apparently, Joseph had learned that telling people about his own dreams could get him *into* trouble, but telling other people about their dreams could get him *out* of trouble.

Before long, Joseph got the attention of Pharaoh, who summoned Joseph to interpret two of Pharaoh's dreams. Pharaoh described watching seven fat, healthy cows grazing along the River Nile, when they were suddenly eaten by seven skinny, sickly cows. Then he had another dream: seven unhealthy, dried-out heads of grain swallowed up seven full, healthy heads of grain.

God gave Joseph the key to those dreams, allowing Joseph to predict what would be happening for the next fourteen years. "Here's what's up," Joseph told Pharaoh. "For the next seven years, Egypt will enjoy bountiful harvests that will produce more than enough grain to feed everyone in Egypt. But seven years of famine will follow those good years—a terrible famine that will cause starvation and death throughout the world."

But Joseph didn't stop when he finished explaining Pharaoh's dreams. Instead, this guy who had just been brought up from the prisons decided he would give some advice to the supreme ruler of Egypt. "Here's what you should do," Joseph said. "Collect a portion of the grain during the abundant years and store it so Egypt will have enough food for the people to survive the seven famine years."

Pharaoh thought that was a fine plan. In fact, he liked it so much that he made Joseph his second-in-command over Egypt, with the job of collecting and storing grain to prepare for the famine, which showed up just as Joseph had predicted. Because of Joseph's foresight, Egypt had plenty of grain stored up to get the Egyptian people through the hard times. Joseph continued as Pharaoh's Golden Boy, living the good life in Egypt for many years to come.

In the Bible, God speaks to his followers in a multitude of ways. Sometimes it's an actual audible voice. Or sometimes it's a physical sign, like a burning bush or a rainbow. And sometimes, God communicates through dreams. For most of us, it's typically a thought or idea that comes to us when we pray that points us in a certain direction or helps us to see a situation in a different light. How do we know if it's God speaking to us versus our minds just playing tricks on us? The best way to confirm the message's origin is to determine whether it lines up with Jesus' teachings and the Lord's plan for our lives.

When we pray, we shouldn't be engaged in a one-way conversation with God. Prayer shouldn't be the equivalent of writing a letter to Santa Claus, listing one request after another. When we communicate with God, we must leave some time for just sitting quietly, with our ears and our hearts open. Give our Lord the opportunity to provide guidance and let us know if we are heading down the right path. Like any good father, he does speak to us, but in his own way and in his own time. We just need to listen.

WHAT DO YOU THINK?

- When Joseph's brothers got angry at Joseph, how should they have expressed their anger—rather than throwing him in a pit or selling him to merchants?
- If Joseph had the chance to do it over again, do you think he would have refrained from describing his dreams to his brothers?
- Has God ever spoken to you? If so, how?
- When you pray, do you leave some quiet time to give the Lord time to communicate with you?

Chapter 12

DREAMS REALLY CAN COME TRUE

(GENESIS 41:46–57; 42; 43:1–14)

The seven years of famine that Joseph predicted happened right on schedule—not only in Egypt, but also well beyond its borders. The famine even reached Canaan, where Jacob and his family were still living. Eventually the family became desperate for food.

Jacob had heard Egypt had plenty of grain for sale, so he told his ten oldest sons to travel there to buy some grain. He kept his youngest and now-favorite son, Benjamin, at home so he wouldn't end up like his brother, Joseph—a midday snack for some wild animal, or the victim of some other calamity. When the ten brothers arrived in Egypt, they were taken right to Joseph, the governor over all the land and the guy in charge of selling the grain. Joseph instantly recognized his brothers, but they had no idea this rich and powerful ruler was the kid they had thrown into a pit many years earlier. It might have been hard for them to get a good look at Joseph anyway, since they were bowing down in front of him and begging him to sell them grain. As it turns out, Joseph's dreams from when he was young did come true.

Joseph, understandably still bitter over having been tossed into a hole in the ground and sold like a bushel of corn, decided to get a little revenge. He said to his brothers: "Where did you come from? I think you must be spies!"

You can bet *that* scared the brothers, so they started telling him lots of details about their family, which is exactly what Joseph wanted. They told him they were all the sons of one father, who was still alive and at home in Canaan with their youngest brother, Benjamin. They also mentioned another brother, who was "no more" (Gen. 42:13). Joseph must have been at least a little bit pleased that they still remembered him at all.

But he wasn't ready to let them off the hook yet, either. Or maybe he was just afraid he would never see them again if he let them all leave with their grain. So Joseph told them the only way they could prove they were not spies would be to go home and bring their youngest brother back with them. No doubt, Joseph knew that convincing their father to let Benjamin return to Egypt would make their lives pretty miserable for a while.

The brothers knew that too, and they began discussing their fate with each other, not knowing that Joseph could understand what they were saying. "This is our punishment for what we did to Joseph," one of them said. "Why were we so mean?" Hearing this, Joseph started to cry, but he turned his face away from his brothers so they couldn't see him weeping. Clearly, Joseph wasn't completely enjoying his brothers' misery. While he apparently had not forgiven them for the way they treated him, he obviously still loved them.

After Joseph regained his composure, he told his brothers he would sell them grain but that he was going to keep one of them, Simeon, in prison in Egypt to make sure they would return with their youngest brother. The brothers left Egypt with full bags of grain but were horrified when they later discovered that all the money they had paid for the grain was back in their sacks. They didn't know that Joseph had secretly ordered his servants to put the money there. We don't know for sure, but Joseph probably couldn't bear the thought of charging his own family for food. Or maybe he just wanted to make his brothers sweat a little more.

When the nine brothers returned home, they told Jacob everything that had happened. Their father was devastated. He started yelling at them like it was all their fault. "You have lost two of my sons already! Do you really think I'm going to let Benjamin out of my sight and go with you?"

But sometime later, when they ran out of food, Jacob knew he had no choice. He had to send his sons back to Egypt to get more grain. And unless they returned with Benjamin, he knew they would not only be denied additional grain, but they could also be prosecuted as spies. So Jacob sent all his remaining sons back with gifts for the Egyptian governor (if he had only known he was sending gifts to his beloved son!) and twice the amount of money to cover both grain purchases.

Poor Jacob knew he could be setting himself up for more heartbreak by sending Benjamin and the others on this trip, so he begged God to spare his sons. As his boys left for Egypt, he said, "May God Almighty give you mercy before the [governor], that he may release to you your other brother and Benjamin" (Gen. 43:14).

Because Joseph's brothers had let anger and jealousy get the best of them, their father was now experiencing deep grief and worry. Joseph's brothers had every right to feel resentful when their father had played favorites with Joseph and every right to be irritated when Joseph described his dreams that seemed to have him lording it over them all. But when they let their anger get completely out of control, they crossed a line that caused everyone—including themselves and their own father—enormous pain and heartache.

In our own lives, there will be times when we believe we are being treated unfairly. And we will know people who brag about their good fortune or accomplishments just a little too much. Sometimes it may even seem like the bad guys are winning. We've all been there, feeling cheated when someone you think is less worthy gets picked for the best position on the baseball field, the front row for the dance performance, or, for the adults, the highest-paying job in the office.

The story of Joseph's brothers shows us how dangerous it can be to nurse a grudge in those situations. It is far better for us to continue to do our best and accept the outcome, even if we don't appreciate the person who wins the prize. That's just the way it is. Spending our time and energy wallowing in anger and plotting our revenge will probably hurt us far more than it hurts the other person. It's difficult to let go of anger or jealousy, but with sincere prayer and God's help, we can be released from those destructive and unpleasant feelings and reach a place of peace and acceptance.

WHAT DO YOU THINK?

- Some people wonder why Joseph's brothers didn't recognize him. Why do you think that could happen?
- In this story, Joseph's brothers learned a valuable lesson about the destructive power of anger and revenge. Do you think Joseph learned a lesson about his own conduct?

Chapter 13

JOSEPH'S BITTERSWEET REVENGE

(GENESIS 43:15–34; 44–45; 46:1–7)

When Jacob's sons arrived in Egypt for their second food-buying trip, they were taken straight to Joseph's house. When Joseph laid eyes on his younger brother, Benjamin, he was overcome with emotion and had to really work to hide his tears so his brothers wouldn't recognize him. Joseph then hosted a big dinner for his brothers in his own home. When it was time for them to leave and head back to Canaan, Joseph ordered that his brothers' bags be filled with as much grain as they could carry and that their money be returned to their sacks—all part of Joseph's plan to torture his brothers one last time.

And then Joseph told his servant to slip Joseph's own silver drinking cup into Benjamin's sack, wait until his brothers were headed home, then track them down and accuse them of stealing it. The servant did as he was told. The brothers loudly denied stealing anything, swearing that the servant would never find the cup among their things. Imagine their shock and dismay when the servant opened Benjamin's bag and pulled out that silver cup!

The brothers returned to Egypt and were brought before Joseph, and the servant reported what had happened. Joseph then ordered Benjamin to stay in Egypt as a slave as punishment for his theft, and he told the other brothers they could go home. But the brothers knew that leaving Benjamin in Egypt would devastate the family, and especially their father. So Judah spoke up and explained to Joseph that Benjamin was one of two sons their father had with his most beloved wife, Rachel. And because the other son "was no more," Jacob loved Benjamin deeply and would surely die of heartbreak if he did not return. "Take me instead," Judah begged, offering to stay in Egypt as a slave if Joseph would just let Benjamin go home.

Joseph couldn't contain his emotion any longer. He ordered all of the Egyptians out of the room so that he could be alone with his brothers. He then burst into tears and exclaimed: "I am your brother, Joseph." At that moment, the brothers were so taken aback they couldn't even speak. But Joseph told them not to be afraid. He said that he would no longer blame them for having him sold as a slave in Egypt. He said, "God sent me before you to preserve for you a remnant in the earth, and to save you alive by a great deliverance. So now it wasn't you who sent me here, but God, and he has made me a father to Pharaoh, lord of all his house, and ruler over all the land of Egypt" (Gen. 45:7–8).

Of course, Joseph's brothers had no idea that selling him into slavery would turn out to be a good thing for their family. No question, their actions were vile. But God had used their sinful plan to work out for good in his bigger plan. Not only was Joseph able to save the Egyptian people from famine, but he also saved his own family from starvation. He told his brothers to go back to Canaan and bring their father and all of their wives and children and all of their livestock to come and live in Goshen, which was known as the best farm land in all of Egypt. "There I will provide for you," Joseph told his brothers, "for there are yet five years of famine; lest you come to poverty, you, and your household, and all that you have" (Gen. 45:11).

So Joseph's brothers went back to Canaan with some unbelievable news for their father: "Joseph is still alive, and he is ruler over all the land of Egypt" (Gen. 45:26). As you might imagine, it took a while before they could convince Jacob they were telling him the truth. But when they did, Jacob was eager to head to Egypt to see his beloved son.

When Jacob finally reunited with Joseph, they hugged for a long time and plenty of tears were shed. "I can die in peace now," Jacob said, "because I know Joseph is alive."

As discussed in chapter 12, the story of Joseph and his brothers shows what can happen when brotherly love becomes infected with jealousy and resentment. But this also is a story about forgiveness. Joseph's love for his family overcame the resentment he felt toward his brothers for how they had treated him. In the end, Joseph was able to move beyond his bitterness by recognizing that even the most horrible part of his life— being sold as a slave and exiled to a foreign land—was part of God's plan that would save the lives of many people, including his entire family.

WHAT DO YOU THINK?

- What finally led Joseph to tell his brothers who he really was?
- After Jacob was reunited with Joseph, do you think he reflected on his own conduct and wondered whether he contributed to the rivalry between his sons that led to Joseph's separation? Do you think he had any regrets?
- The story of Joseph and his brothers is one of history's most magnificent tales of revenge, redemption, and ultimately forgiveness. Have you ever had to forgive someone for something terrible that they did to you? How did you find the strength to forgive?
- Is there someone you have not been able to forgive?

Chapter 14

BABY MOSES: THE NILE RETURNS THE FAVOR TO PHARAOH

(EXODUS 1–3; 4:1–19)

Jacob and his family lived a happy life in Egypt, enjoying the benefits of Joseph's close relationship with Pharaoh. When Joseph and his brothers all died, their kids and grandkids stayed in Egypt, where the farming was easy and their families just kept growing. However, over the course of many generations, conditions for the Israelites deteriorated dramatically.

Unfortunately, when people live under the rule of a different ethnic or religious group, they are often mistreated. Eventually, the Egyptians forgot all about Joseph and how he had helped their country, and they enslaved the Israelite or "Hebrew" people, the descendants of Jacob and Joseph. One particularly paranoid Pharaoh became convinced that the Israelite population in Egypt had grown so big that it was threatening his power. So he ordered all newborn Hebrew boys to be killed and thrown into the Nile River.

One Israelite woman, Jochebed, managed to keep her baby son hidden for the first few months of his life. But when the baby became too big and too noisy to hide, Jochebed hatched a new plan for saving his life. She made a basket out of papyrus reeds and tar and then placed the baby into the basket and floated him at the edge of the Nile among the reeds. It's not clear why she thought releasing her infant son onto an enormous river would increase his chances of survival, but her plan actually worked.

Jochebed's daughter, Miriam, hid behind some bushes to watch what would happen to her floating baby brother. While she was hiding, Pharaoh's daughter came down to bathe in the river and was intrigued by the floating basket. When she opened the basket and found a crying baby, her heart melted, even though she knew this was a Hebrew baby that her father had said should be put to death.

Pharaoh's daughter took the baby out of the basket and into her arms. Miriam then popped out of the bushes and offered to make herself useful. "Should I go and call a nurse for you from the Hebrew women, that she may nurse the child for you?" (Ex. 2:7). Pharaoh's daughter gladly accepted her offer, so Miriam ran off and found the perfect nurse for the baby: Jochebed.

Of course, Jochebed was thrilled that her son was now being protected by Pharaoh's daughter and even more thrilled to get a chance to stay close to the baby for a while. Pharaoh's daughter claimed the baby as her own son and named him Moses, which means "to pull out of," as in, pulled out of the Nile.

As Moses grew older, he moved into Pharaoh's palace to live with his adopted Egyptian family. One day, when he was all grown up, he saw an Egyptian taskmaster beating a Hebrew slave. Probably feeling his connection to the slave, Moses became so out-raged that he attacked the Egyptian taskmaster, killed him, and buried him in the sand. Moses thought he had committed his deed in secret, but his actions didn't stay secret for long. Pharaoh learned about it and ordered that Moses be killed for his crime. But Moses escaped, running away from Egypt to a land out in the desert called Midian.

Life in Midian was kind to Moses. He met a woman named Zipporah, married her, had two sons, and settled down to his life as a shepherd, taking care of the sheep belonging to his father-in-law, Jethro. One day, Moses was out in the wilderness herding sheep when he spotted a bush burning in the distance. He moved closer and realized the bush was engulfed in flames but wasn't being charred or consumed.

God then called out to him from the middle of the bush. "Moses! Moses!" And Moses answered, "Here I am" (Ex. 3:4). As if carrying on a conversation with a big, flaming plant wasn't strange enough, things got even weirder for Moses when the burning bush started ordering him around: "Don't get too close," it warned. "And take off your sandals; that's not just any patch of desert right there—it's holy ground." Moses did as he was told. Then, the bush finally identified itself. "I am the God of your father, the God of Abraham, the God of Isaac, and the God of Jacob" (Ex. 3:6).

Hearing that, Moses became REALLY scared. He hid his face and wouldn't even look at the bush. So God got down to business. The Lord explained to Moses that the Hebrew people in Egypt were still suffering under Pharaoh and God had decided it was time to put an end to that suffering. "So, get yourself together, Moses, and get back to Egypt and set my people free."

By this point, Moses probably wished he had never stumbled upon this burning bush. "You want me to what? Let me get this straight. You're telling me to march on up to Pharaoh, right there in that big, fancy palace of his, and tell him that he needs to release the thousands of Hebrews he's using as slaves? Why me?"

"Well, I'm not sending you alone, Moses," God responded. "I'll be going with you. You just tell Pharaoh and all my people that the I AM sent you."

Moses still wasn't convinced. "Of all the people in the world you could have picked for this job, why did you pick me? Need I remind you that I killed a man in Egypt and that Pharaoh wants to kill me? Thanks for the honor of choosing me, but I think I'll pass."

Of course, Moses wasn't quite so blunt because he understood that you don't get snotty with the creator of the universe, particularly when he's talking to you through a raging ball of flames. Instead, Moses tried to make lots of excuses. For example, he told God that he was an awkward speaker and that God should pick, for this most important task, someone who had the gift of gab. God kept swatting away those excuses with miraculous signs and pledges of support. The Lord even promised to recruit Aaron, Moses' smooth-talking brother, into the crusade. Eventually, Moses realized that "no" wasn't an option, and he started making preparations for his journey.

Reading about Moses' divine encounter reminds us that we can often be baffled by who the Lord selects to carry out his divine plans. Moses appeared to be the most unlikely candidate to deliver God's message to Pharaoh. First, he would be betraying his adopted Egyptian mother by demanding the release of all the Hebrew slaves because their loss could devastate Pharaoh's kingdom. Also, let's not forget that Moses was a fugitive from justice who was guilty of killing an Egyptian. And, to top it all off, the guy was entirely unable to speak with even a shred of eloquence. Yet God chose Moses to speak on his behalf to bring about the freedom of the Hebrew people.

Like Moses, we may sometimes sense that God wants us to step up and do something we feel unqualified to do. It might be fulfilling a leadership role in the church. Or it could be refusing to follow the crowd in some very visible way. Or taking a public stand to defend your Christian beliefs. We often hear God's call when we know that it will be inconvenient or embarrassing to answer him. Sometimes answering seems impossible. But the story of Moses teaches us that when the Lord comes calling, he will equip us with whatever we need to get the job done.

Answering God's call and fulfilling the mission he gives us will not always be easy. But it will always be doable. And when we rise to the challenge, we will grow and become stronger and more resilient Christians. We also will receive the wonderful blessings that come from fulfilling God's purpose for our lives.

WHAT DO YOU THINK?

- Why did God choose to speak to Moses through a fiery bush? Why do you think the bush was not consumed by the flames?
- If Aaron was a much better speaker than Moses, why didn't God just pick Aaron to deliver the message to Pharaoh? Why was Moses the right choice?
- Have you ever been called to do a job you felt unqualified for? Did you ask God for help? Did God help you through it?

Chapter 15

LOCUSTS AND SKIN BOILS AND FROGS, OH MY!

(EXODUS 4:20–31; 5–11; 12:1–32)

After Moses quit arguing with God, he gathered up his family and headed back to Egypt, preparing to confront Pharaoh about releasing the Hebrew slaves. First, Moses and his brother, Aaron, met with the Israelite elders and explained why Moses had returned and what he was planning to do. Moses even performed some miraculous signs, just like God told him to, so the Israelites could be sure this wasn't some little scheme Moses had cooked up on his own.

Then Moses and Aaron headed to Pharaoh's palace to deliver God's message. "Pharaoh, we have a message for you. Yahweh, the God of Israel, says, 'Let my people go' so they can hold a feast for me out in the wilderness." (The Israelite people often used the name of Yahweh when they talked about God.)

Pharaoh was not amused. "I don't even know that god. Why should I listen to him? What are you doing in my palace anyway? If you Israelites have time to dream about feasts out in the wilderness, you must not have enough work to do. I'll take care of that!"

So Pharaoh told his slave masters to stop giving the Hebrew slaves straw, which was a key ingredient the Israelites needed for making bricks. But the Israelites would still be required to make the same number of bricks per day. This freedom thing did not seem to be working out too well for the Israelites, and they complained to Moses. "I don't know what you said to Pharaoh, but we are worse off now than we were before you showed up here. Are you sure you saw God in that bush?"

Moses was horrified, and he took their complaints to God. "Lord, why have you brought trouble on this people? Why is it that you have sent me? For since I came to Pharaoh to speak in your name, he has brought trouble on this people. You have not rescued your people at all" (Ex. 5:22).

But God was just getting started. "Now you shall see what I will do to Pharaoh," he told Moses, "for by a strong hand he shall let them go, and by a strong hand he shall drive them out of his land" (Ex. 6:1).

So Moses went back to Pharaoh and again demanded that he let the Israelites leave Egypt. As God had instructed, Aaron threw his staff on the ground, and everyone jumped back when it turned into a snake. But Pharaoh wasn't impressed. He just called in his magicians to do the same trick with their staffs. But then, Pharaoh nearly fell off his jewel-studded throne when Aaron's snake swallowed up the others.

However, a bit of snake magic was not enough to get Pharaoh to agree to let the Hebrew people go free, which did not surprise God. He told Moses and the Israelites not to worry; he was working on something really big. "I will lay my hand on Egypt, and bring out my armies, my people the children of Israel, out of the land of Egypt by great judgments. The Egyptians shall know that I am Yahweh when I stretch out my hand on Egypt, and bring the children of Israel out from among them" (Ex. 7:4–5).

RANK THE PLAGUES

So God ordered ten horrific plagues on Egypt to show Pharaoh who was boss and to convince him to release the Jewish people. The first nine were pretty terrible, and the tenth was absolutely devastating—more on that one later. Instead of telling you all about the first nine plagues in the order in which they actually occurred, I thought it might be more interesting to discuss them from least dire to most dreadful, at least in my opinion.

9. Flies. Flies can be incredibly annoying. And God didn't send just a few flies to ruin the Egyptians' backyard barbecues. He sent swarms of flies on Pharaoh and his people to make their lives miserable. However, I do get enormous satisfaction out of whacking flies with my fly swatter. So, because they do provide at least some entertainment value, I put the plague of flies at the number nine spot as the least objectionable of the group.

8. Three days of total darkness. Whenever we have a power failure at our house, an hour seems like an eternity. And the Bible tells us this darkness was so "thick" that the Egyptians couldn't even "see one another" (Ex. 10:22–23). Three full days of pitch blackness must have been scary, not to mention totally boring, especially since the Egyptians had no idea when it would end, which probably made it seem even longer. But compared to some of the other plagues, this one seems relatively low on the "unbearable" spectrum.

7. Locusts. I have fond memories of lying in bed during warm, summer nights in late August when I was a kid, listening to the peaceful hum of locusts outside. But the locusts of this plague didn't just hang out and provide pleasant background noise. They covered "the surface of the earth" and ate "every tree" in the field. And some of them headed indoors, filling the homes of the Egyptians like no one had ever seen before (Ex. 10:5–6). But I still get nostalgic when I think about locusts, so I ranked this plague fairly low on the devastating scale.

6. Pestilence on the livestock. I'm not a vegetarian or vegan, but I do have sympathy for animals. So I scored this plague a six because a lot of poor animals suffered and died even though they never bothered anyone and couldn't tell Pharaoh to let the Israelites go.

5. All the water in Egypt turned to blood. Don't forget, this plague happened before they invented Gatorade. So, unless you're Count Dracula, having nothing to drink but blood would be pretty gross. Even putting aside the personal dehydration factor, being unable to bathe, wash your clothes, or wash your car (or, back then, your camel) would be rough.

4. Lice. When our twins were around five years old, they got head lice and passed it on to my wife, Catherine, and me. Catherine wasn't keen on putting harsh chemicals on our heads and insisted we deploy an organic method of ridding ourselves of the pests. So, every night before we went to bed, we drenched our hair in olive oil and covered it with a plastic shower cap, hoping the little boogers would suffocate to death while we slept. I remember lying awake one hot night as oil trickled down the side of my face onto my pillow. I felt like my head was a giant, sweaty crouton hermetically sealed inside a Caesar salad. It was awful. That's why I ranked this plague probably higher on the misery scale than other people might.

3. Frogs. I actually like frogs, so I first thought this plague could have been kinda fun. But then I kept reading: "The river will swarm with frogs, which will go up and come into your house, and into your bedroom, and on your bed … and into your ovens, and into your kneading troughs" (Ex. 8:3). As much as I like frogs, I definitely don't want them hopping around in my bed at night. And I certainly don't want them jumping out of my Rice Krispies in the morning. So this one earns a solid number three.

2. Thunderstorms of hail. Even relatively mild hailstorms can be destructive. But the one that God sent down on Egypt was over the top: "The hail struck throughout all the land of Egypt all that was in the field, both man and animal; and the hail struck every herb of the field, and broke every tree of the field" (Ex. 9:15). If the hail was strong enough to destroy trees, it easily could have decimated a human being. So this one gets second place.

And, now, for the coveted number one spot. Drumroll please …

1. Skin boils! Boils cause serious pain and physical suffering, and you also have to consider the ugliness factor. Even the most powerful zit cream on earth would be no match for the Lord Almighty's epidermal masterpieces. So this one wins for my pick of the nastiest of the first nine plagues—a dubious honor indeed.

THE TENTH AND FINAL PLAGUE

God imposed these nine plagues one torturous episode at a time. Each time the plague seemed unbearable, Pharaoh would summon Moses, beg him to ask God to call off the misery, and promise to let the Hebrew people go free. But as soon as God removed the plague, Pharaoh would go back on his promise. God, Pharaoh, and Moses repeated this little scene nine times.

Finally, God prepared to unleash the most devastating plague of all: the death of the firstborn son of every Egyptian family. First, the Lord gave Moses instructions to guarantee that Israelite families would be protected from this plague. All of the Hebrew families sacrificed a lamb and painted their doorposts with the blood of the lamb. That blood told God's angel of death to "pass over" their homes, sparing the firstborn Israelite boys. God also told the Israelites to be packed and ready to leave their homes at a moment's notice, even in the middle of the night. He knew that after years of slavery, the Israelites would become free in the blink of an eye.

Sure enough, that night, God "struck all the firstborn in the land of Egypt, from the firstborn of Pharaoh who sat on his throne to the firstborn of the captive who was in the dungeon, and all the firstborn of livestock. Pharaoh rose up in the night, he, and all his servants, and all the Egyptians; and there was a great cry in Egypt, for there was not a house where there was not one dead" (Ex. 12:29–30).

Pharaoh was so upset that he called Moses and Aaron in the middle of the night. He not only gave the Israelites permission to go, he actually ordered them to leave. "Get out of here! Take your wives and your kids and your sheep and cows and leave!"

The liberation of the Israelites from Egypt remains a vital part of the history, religion, and culture of the Jewish people to this day. Passover is celebrated every year, commemorating the night that God passed over Jewish homes and rained death upon the Egyptians, prompting Pharaoh to free the Israelites.

The Passover story reminds us in very stark terms that nobody on earth is higher than the one and only true God, our Creator in heaven. Pharaoh, a mere mortal, believed he was the ultimate ruler of the world and that he answered to no one. He was so convinced of his own preeminence that it took ten plagues and the death of his own son before he would admit that he was powerless in the face of Yahweh, the God of Israel.

In some ways, we all are a bit like Pharaoh. When we're riding high and on top of the world, we're convinced that our good fortune is the result of our birthright, or our ingenuity, or our talent, or our hard work. During those times, we refuse to acknowledge that everything good and everything worthwhile comes from the Lord. But God loves us enough to sometimes let life's adversities smack us in the face as a wake-up call, to remind us that he is the source of our strength, our success, and our hope for the future.

Our adversities can force us to our knees and beg God to grant us relief from the pain. But sometimes, like Pharaoh, we forget what we learned as soon as our troubles are taken away, and we put God back on the shelf. For many of us, the cycle repeats itself over and over again. But we can break the cycle if we remain close to God, study his word, and communicate with him regularly through worship and prayer. Only then will life's challenges no longer tear us down. Instead, they will mold and shape us into the strong, courageous, humble, and honorable people that God wants us to be.

WHAT DO YOU THINK?

• Do you think the Jewish elders were worried about Moses approaching Pharaoh? What could they have been thinking and feeling?

• After God lifted each of the plagues, how do you think Pharaoh justified changing his mind and not allowing the Israelite people to go free?

• Have you ever acted like Pharaoh? That is, have you ever promised to change something when you realized the consequences of your bad actions but later gone back to that same behavior?

• What are your top two picks for the worst of the plagues? Which one do you think would be the easiest to endure?

Chapter 16

WE ARE *SO* OUTTA HERE!

(EXODUS 12:33–51; 13–14)

The Israelites had lived in Egypt for more than 400 years when they were finally able to say goodbye to it, once and for all, as free people. And the Egyptians, who had suffered and lost so much during the ten plagues, were more than happy to see the Israelite people leave. The Egyptians even gave the Israelites gold and silver jewelry and clothing—anything just to get rid of these people!

The Israelites had been preparing for a hasty exit. They didn't even wait for the dough in their bread to rise, so they carried it on their backs, letting it bake in the sun. The net result? A large flat cracker. The Lord then commanded that the Israelites remember this time every year, celebrating a week of Passover while eating only unleavened bread, or matzah, so that they would never forget how they had to rush out of Egypt for their long-awaited exodus.

The Israelites ventured out into the desert in search of the Promised Land—the region of Canaan "flowing with milk and honey" that God had promised to their forefathers, Abraham, Isaac, and Jacob (Ex. 13:5). As the Jewish people traveled beyond the outskirts of Egypt and into unfamiliar territory, the Lord guided them through the desert with a "pillar of cloud" during the day and a "pillar of fire" at night (Ex. 13:21–22).

But the Israelites had not been gone from Egypt for very long when Pharaoh had a change of heart and regretted letting them go. So he gathered up his army, hitched up his fastest horses to his speediest chariots, and charged out in hot pursuit of the Hebrew people. The Israelites were camping at the shore of the Red Sea when they heard the sound of pounding horse hooves and saw Pharaoh and his army storming toward them, ready to attack.

Terrified, the people turned on Moses. "You brought us out here to die! We're trapped; there's nowhere to run and no way we can fight that army that's coming! We are going to be slaughtered in the desert by Pharaoh and his army."

But Moses reassured them that God had not finished with his miracles. "Don't be afraid. Stand still, and see the salvation of Yahweh, which he will work for you today; for you will never again see the Egyptians whom you have seen today. Yahweh will fight for you, and you shall be still" (Ex. 14:13–14).

And the Lord did hear the cries of the Israelite people. He moved the pillar of cloud between the Hebrew people and Pharaoh's men to block the Egyptian army from approaching. Moses then raised his staff in the direction of the Red Sea, as God had commanded, and the Lord brought a strong wind from the east that blew all night long and divided the sea in two. A dry path appeared through the Red Sea, with a wall of water standing on either side.

The Israelites rushed across the dry land, marveling at the walls of water piled up on either side of them. Then God removed the pillars of cloud and fire, and Pharaoh and his men charged down the path in the sea toward Moses and his people. But God caused the wheels to fall off their chariots and stirred up confusion, and some of the Egyptian soldiers got scared and wanted to turn back.

But by that point, the Israelites had all reached dry ground on the other side of the Red Sea, so Moses turned and faced Pharaoh and again raised his staff. And God sent the walls of water crashing down over Pharaoh and his army. Exodus 14:28 says, "The waters returned, and covered the chariots and the horsemen, even all Pharaoh's army that went in after them into the sea. There remained not so much as one of them."

Safe and secure on the other side of the Red Sea, the Israelites watched the bodies of the Egyptians wash onto shore and knew that God had saved them that day from the hand of the Egyptians. "Israel saw the great work which Yahweh did to the Egyptians, and the people feared Yahweh; and they believed in Yahweh and in his servant Moses" (Ex. 14:31).

Of course, this dramatic event convinced the Israelites that the Lord was on their side, watching over them, and would keep them safe no matter what challenges they might face out in the desert. But how long would their sense of safety and their conviction in God's protection last? Well, keep reading.

WHAT DO YOU THINK?

• Describe some of the real-world, practical challenges the Israelites likely faced when they left their homes and started walking out into the wilderness.

• After watching God's many miracles leading up to their exodus, why would the Israelites doubt that God would take care of them when Pharaoh and his army approached?

• Why do you think God brought such a violent end to Pharaoh and his army?

Chapter 17

HEY LORD, WHAT HAVE YOU DONE FOR ME LATELY?

(EXODUS 16; 17:1–7; 19–32; NUMBERS 20:1–13)

While the Israelites were celebrating their exodus out of Egypt and their miraculous passage across the Red Sea, they had no way of knowing they were embarking on a journey across the wilderness that would last forty years and be filled with one harrowing experience after another. Unfortunately, when things got rough on this seemingly endless trek through some very unforgiving terrain, the Israelites tended to lose faith and give in to complaining and fear. Fortunately, the Lord never gave up on them, even though he did make them face some harsh consequences at times.

Let's take a look at some of the hardships the Israelites faced, how they reacted to those difficulties, and how God carried them through.

HUNGER

Not too long after they left Egypt, the Israelites were running out of food and getting hungry.

Their reaction. The Israelites griped bitterly about not having enough food. And, just like when Pharaoh's army was closing in on them, they blamed Moses for even bringing them out of Egypt in the first place. "Yeah, we were slaves, but at least we had meat and bread in Egypt," they whined. "What was the point of all this, just so we could starve to death out here in the wilderness?"

God's solution. God told Moses that he had heard the grumblings and was getting another miracle ready. He passed along a message for Moses to deliver to the people: "At evening you shall eat meat, and in the morning you shall be filled with bread. Then you will know that I am Yahweh your God" (Ex. 16:12). That evening, the Lord sent so many quail that they covered the camp, giving the Israelites their fill of meat.

And starting the next morning, God rained down bread from heaven, which he called manna. It "was like coriander seed, white; and its taste was like wafers with honey" (Ex. 16:31), and it showed up six days a week. The people were ordered to pick up just enough for everyone in their family to have food for the day because the manna would not stay edible for more than one day. EXCEPT on Fridays. No manna would fall on Saturday, the Sabbath day, so families had to pick up enough manna on Fridays to last them for two days, and that manna lasted just fine. Manna didn't fall on the Sabbath so the Israelites would not have to work on the Lord's day of rest.

THIRST

Not too long after God worked out the hunger problem, the Israelites were having trouble finding water.

Their reaction. They turned on Moses again, this time asking him: "Why have you brought us up out of Egypt, to kill us, our children, and our livestock with thirst?" (Ex. 17:3). The people were so furious with Moses that he was afraid they would stone him to death.

God's solution. The Lord led Moses to a rock in the region of Horeb and instructed him to take his staff and strike the rock. Moses did as he was told, and water flowed from the rock, giving the Israelite people plenty of water for themselves and their livestock.

FEELINGS OF ABANDONMENT

The Israelites eventually made their way through the wilderness to Mount Sinai, camping at the foot of the mountain. God ordered Moses to climb on up for a conversation. Seems like the Lord wanted Moses' undivided attention because he was planning to give him the Ten Commandments—the ten fundamental rules the Israelites should follow—and a lot of other laws and rules. God engraved the Ten Commandments with his finger onto two stone tablets for Moses to carry down to the people. The Lord also gave Moses plans for building a tabernacle and the Ark of the Covenant, which was an ornate wooden chest that the Jewish people would use to house various sacred objects, including the stone tablets that bore the Ten Commandments. Moses was up on that mountain with God for forty days and forty nights.

Their reaction. Moses was on the mountain for such a long time that the Israelites began to panic, thinking he was gone for good. They confronted Aaron, Moses' brother, and demanded he create godly images to take Moses' place in leading them on their journey. The people then gathered all of their gold jewelry and brought it to Aaron, who melted it down and formed a golden calf. The Israelites then bowed down, worshiped it, and made sacrifices to it.

God's solution. The Lord grew enraged when he saw what the Israelites were doing, and he sent Moses back down the mountain, where he found the people dancing and celebrating around the golden calf. Moses became so furious that he smashed the stone tablets that bore the Ten Commandments and destroyed the golden calf, ground it up into powder and sprinkled it in the drinking water. Later, Moses returned to the mountain for another forty days, and God gave him a new set of stone tablets engraved with his commandments. This time, the Israelites seemed to be content to wait for Moses to return.

THIRST, THE SEQUEL

Many decades later, when the Israelites had been wandering around the desert for almost forty years, they settled in the region of Zin and again found themselves without water.

Their reaction. They griped to Moses and Aaron (who else?) and again wondered why they had ever left Egypt. "Why have you made us to come up out of Egypt, to bring us in to this evil place? It is no place of seed, or of figs, or of vines, or of pomegranates; neither is there any water to drink" (Num. 20:5).

God's solution. The Lord told Moses and Aaron to gather the people together in front of a rock at nearby Meribah. God then gave Moses specific instructions on what to do next: Moses must speak to the rock. However, Moses didn't quite follow the Lord's instructions. After gathering the Israelites in front of the rock, he yelled at them and called them "rebels." Then Moses turned around and whacked the rock twice, and water poured out of it, giving the people all they needed for themselves and their animals.

ONE IMPORTANT SIDE-NOTE

God was not happy that Moses did not follow his clear and specific orders on how to get water from this stone. He said that when Moses refused to speak to the rock, yelled at the people, and then struck the rock with his staff, he had demonstrated a lack of faith and robbed the Lord of the glory he had earned. So God told Moses he would not be permitted to enter the Promised Land with the Israelites.

SLOW LEARNERS

Nobody would ever accuse the Israelites of suffering in silence. Or of being too trusting. No matter how many times God rescued them from the calamity *du jour*, whenever the next crisis arose, the Israelites invariably would abandon any hope that God would take care of them and start whining about dying a horrific death in the desert. Then they would blame Moses for the whole darn mess.

When God fended off Pharaoh's army, rained food down on them from heaven, or poured water out of a desert stone, the

Israelites gladly accepted the blessing. But they never seemed to utter a single word of gratitude, just got back to business until the next round of trouble reared its ugly head.

While it would be easy to judge the Hebrew people for their lack of faith and gratitude, aren't we all guilty of doing the same thing? Many times, we cry out to the Lord when we face moments of crisis. But no sooner does God answer our prayers and help us through the trouble, than we quickly move on with barely a word of thanks. It's not much different from what happened with Pharaoh. But Pharaoh kept forgetting the lessons he learned from God's rebukes. The Israelites were forgetting the lessons learned from God's blessings.

When it comes to God's interventions in our lives, our memories can be short. But, as the Lord's followers, we need to develop longer attention spans and bigger memory banks. We grow spiritually when we express ongoing gratitude to the Lord and dwell on his many divine intercessions in our lives. Build a treasure trove of memories about the times when God has rescued you from trouble or helped you make it through a hard time. Then, when that moment comes and you must confront the next challenge or hardship, your faith in God will remain strong and you will take comfort in knowing that the Lord will carry you through.

WHAT DO YOU THINK?

- Imagine that you are charged with defending the Jewish people before God. How can you convince God not to judge them too harshly for griping so much? What would your best arguments be?
- Now, imagine you are God, responding to those arguments. What points do you think God would make?
- Do you think God was too harsh when he punished Moses for not following his instructions at the rock at Meribah? Why do you think God imposed such an extreme consequence?
- Can you think of times when God helped you through a personal crisis and you forgot to thank him?

Chapter 18

ARE WE THERE YET? (THE ROAD TRIP FROM HELL)

(NUMBERS 13; 14:1–35; DEUTERONOMY 34)

In the last chapter, we saw that the Israelites' journey in the desert was long and grueling. Why would God put his chosen people through the wringer for another forty years after they had suffered for so many years as slaves in Egypt? Well, there actually was a good reason for that.

About a year after the Israelites had escaped Egypt, the Lord led them to the outskirts of Canaan, the land flowing with milk and honey that God had promised to Abraham and his descendants. God instructed Moses to send scouts (spies) into Canaan to get a sense of the land and the people who inhabited it. Moses appointed one scout from each of the twelve tribes of Israel and instructed the twelve men to gather information on Canaan.

The twelve scouts spent forty days in the region and came back with some good news and a lot of bad news. They raved about the fertile land and all the great food growing there, such as grapes, pomegranates, and figs. Then they started talking about the people. Ten of the scouts reported that the people who lived in

Canaan were big, strong, and scary—actual giants—living in cities protected by thick walls. "They're stronger than we are," the scouts said. "And so big, we felt like grasshoppers compared to them!"

These ten scouts were afraid the Israelites would be slaughtered if they invaded this land. "I know God wants us to go live in Canaan, but maybe we can find us a nice patch of desert where we can settle down somewhere else," they said.

Two brave scouts had a different opinion: Caleb, from the tribe of Judah, and Joshua, from the tribe of Ephraim. Caleb spoke up first. "Don't be so afraid," he argued. "If God fights for us, we can beat anyone! Remember the Red Sea?"

But the Israelites had already been frightened and they turned on their favorite punching bags: Moses and Aaron. "We wish that we had died in the land of Egypt, or that we had died in this wilderness! Why does Yahweh bring us to this land, to fall by the sword? Our wives and our little ones will be captured or killed! Wouldn't it be better for us to return into Egypt?" (Num. 14:3). They even started talking about picking out a leader to take them back to Egypt.

Not surprisingly, the Lord was furious that the Israelites had rejected his plan and at their complete lack of faith that he would keep them safe. He even suggested to Moses that he would just wipe out the entire nation and start a new one from Moses' family. Moses convinced God that wouldn't be such a good idea, so the Lord instead declared that the Israelites would wander through the desert for another forty years before entering the Promised Land: one year for each day that the scouts spent in Canaan. *And none of the Israelites over the age of twenty would live to enter the Promised Land, except Caleb and Joshua.*

God was true to his word. The Israelites spent another forty years traveling in circles through the wilderness, while almost the whole adult population died from various causes. Only Caleb and Joshua survived to enter Canaan.

Moses lost his chance to enter into the Promised Land because of the way he handled the water situation at the rock at Meribah. But God took Moses to the top of Mount Nebo just as the Israelites were finally getting ready to enter Canaan and let him look out over the land. Moses died on that mountaintop, and God buried him, and no humans ever knew where. Moses was 120 years old by that time.

Many people who read the biblical account of Moses' life think God was far too harsh with Moses, especially because Moses had endured so much over his long life to fulfill God's plan for his people. They argue that Moses' banishment from the Promised Land didn't fit the crime, that it was too severe, that it was unfair. However, it is not our place to second-guess the decisions of our Lord and Creator. We have to believe he has his reasons.

Maybe there is more to the story than what is provided in the biblical account. It's possible that Moses' conduct at Meribah was just one of several occasions on which Moses, in his later years, went against God's authority. Or perhaps denying Moses entry into Canaan wasn't such a big deal for Moses. For all we know, maybe Moses wasn't a fan of milk or honey. Or maybe he was lactose-intolerant and on a low-carb diet, so milk and honey would have made him both sick and chubby at the same time. We'll never know for sure.

But the Bible makes crystal clear that the Lord loved Moses dearly. Although I can't pretend to know the mind of God, I like to think that God pulled the curtain on Moses' life as an act of love. I suspect that Moses was ready for his final rest by the time the Israelites reached Canaan the second time around. And the Israelites weren't going to just waltz into the Promised Land and live happily ever after. The people were about to face many fierce battles to secure their claim to the region. Moses may have been quite content to pass the torch to his successor, Joshua, to lead his people into battle.

Moses must have been happy viewing Canaan from on high, knowing that his people would finally enter the land promised to their forefathers. As he sat atop Mount Nebo, Moses must have felt that he fought the good fight and was ready to receive the ultimate reward for his devotion to God: joining our Heavenly Father in a place of eternal joy and peace.

WHAT DO YOU THINK?

- The scouts that Moses sent into Canaan were there for forty days. That number comes up a lot, doesn't it? Do you think that's just a coincidence?

- Based on everything that you have read so far in this book, what three adjectives would you use to describe God? Keep those words in mind and consider if they change as you read the rest of the book, especially the stories from the New Testament.

- God punished his people by making them wander in the wilderness for forty years. Do you think those years might have served other purposes for God?

- Imagine you were with Moses as he sat atop Mount Nebo looking out onto the Promised Land. What one question would you like to ask him?

Chapter 19

FORGET THE BATTERING RAM; WE NEED BUGLES!

(JOSHUA 1–6)

The Israelites' long journey through the desert was finally coming to an end. They were camped just east of the Jordan River, with nothing standing between them and the Promised Land except this historic body of water where, over a thousand years later, Jesus would be baptized. At long last, the Hebrew people were returning to the land that God had pledged to their forefathers, the land where hundreds of years earlier, Isaac and Rebekah had raised their sons, Jacob and Esau. Later in his life, Jacob left Canaan with his eleven sons and their families, headed to Egypt to wait out the famine. Now, his descendants were returning, thousands upon thousands of them—ready to claim their promised land.

The Lord had appointed Joshua, who had been Moses' right-hand man, to lead the Israelites into Canaan. It was a big job, but Joshua would have divine help. "Be strong and courageous," God told Joshua. "Don't be afraid. Don't be dismayed, for Yahweh your God is with you wherever you go" (Josh. 1:9).

Before the Israelites crossed into Canaan, Joshua wanted to know more about this unfamiliar region, especially Jericho, the first major city they would encounter. Jericho was famous for the mighty wall that surrounded it on all sides. So Joshua sent two spies to sneak into the city and gather information.

Somehow, the king of Jericho learned of their presence and ordered them to be arrested. But a woman named Rahab hid them in her home and protected them. The information gathered by the men on Jericho that would prove most useful was not the height of its walls, the number of men in its army, or the size of its stockpile of weapons. Instead, it was what Rahab told them about the people of Jericho: that they were terrified of the Israelites. The people of Jericho had heard how the Lord parted the Red Sea and vanquished Pharaoh's army. They also knew that God had taken care of the Israelites in the wilderness and was still protecting his people.

Rahab proposed a deal to the two men. She would continue hiding and protecting them if the Israelites would spare her and her family when they conquered the city. It sounded like a good deal to the spies, so they agreed.

Rahab lived in a house built on top of the wall of Jericho, and she threw a rope out her window that night so the two spies could climb down and escape. When the two men returned to the Israelite camp, they reported to Joshua everything they had seen and heard—and the people were especially excited to know that the Canaanites were already terrified.

At God's command, Joshua ordered the chief priests to carry the Ark of the Covenant to the edge of the Jordan River, with all the people of Israel following behind. As soon as the feet of the priests dipped into the water's edge, God parted the river, just as he had done to the Red Sea decades earlier. The nation of Israel passed through the river unharmed. If the people of Jericho were scared before, they were really worried now!

With the Jordan River in their rearview mirror, the Israelites approached Jericho and its towering walls, a major roadblock to their passage into the heart of Canaan. How should they fight this battle? Attack the walls with a battering ram? Shoot flaming arrows over it? Scale it with ropes and ladders? God had a different plan.

God ordered Joshua to give trumpets made of rams' horns to seven priests and to deliver God's marching orders. For six days, the priests blew those horns while marching around the walls of Jericho as the Israelite fighting forces marched behind them in total silence. Several men carried the Ark of the Covenant in the back of the procession. You have to wonder what the citizens of Jericho were thinking, as they hid inside their walls, preparing for an attack, while the Israelites just marched around the city and blew on some horns.

The seventh day started out much like the first six, with the priests blowing their horns and the fighting men marching behind them. But this day, the Israelites didn't go back to camp after one lap around the city. They kept going, circling Jericho seven times. And on the seventh circle around, the fighting men started making noise too—yelling, whooping, and hollering as they marched, terrifying the confused people of Jericho.

And, as the priests blew their horns and the Israelite men shouted, the walls of Jericho crashed down, and the Israelite men poured straight into the city. The people of Jericho were so afraid of the Israelites and the God who protected them that they never really defended themselves. So the Israelites quite easily conquered Jericho and burned it to the ground—but not before rescuing Rahab and her family, just as the spies had promised.

The book of Joshua tells us that the number of Jewish men who were ready for battle against Jericho was about 40,000 (Josh. 4:13). But it wasn't the size or strength of the army or how many weapons they carried that allowed them to conquer the city. Their success came because Joshua and the Israelites followed God's instructions down to the most minor detail. No military leader would ever choose to march around a walled city for a week before attacking. In the ancient world, armies would build ramps or towers to go over the walls, or tunnel underneath them, or use battering rams to knock down the city gates. But Joshua and his people trusted God and obediently followed his instructions even when they seemed absurd. Because they obeyed, the Israelites got quick and easy access to the city and a resounding victory.

As the Israelites moved beyond Jericho and deeper into the heart of Canaan, they engaged in many battles over a number of years in their quest to conquer this territory. When they remained obedient to God, the Israelites were successful and eventually controlled the vast majority of the entire region. When they disobeyed God or forgot to ask for his instructions in certain cases, they often suffered defeats. Thankfully, these losses were less frequent than the victories.

Just like God instructed Joshua on how to attack Jericho, the Lord also directs us on how to address the challenges in our own lives. His guidance might come to us during times of prayer, at Bible study, or through the teachings we receive in church.

Sometimes God's directives come to us when we're out for a walk, daydreaming in school, or lying in bed before we fall asleep.

God's plan of action doesn't always align with our own, and it might even look illogical sometimes. For example, he might encourage us to put the books aside on a Sunday so that we can attend church, even if we have a big final the next day. Or he might direct us to leave a relationship with someone because that person would turn out to be toxic to our spiritual health.

We need to bear in mind that the Lord sees the full picture—present, past, and future—that isn't always visible to the rest of us. We must trust in him and follow his guidance just as the Israelites did in the Promised Land. If we do, we will be victorious in our own battles, achieve greatness, and receive the blessings the Lord bestows upon those who are obedient to him.

WHAT DO YOU THINK?

- What does the battle of Jericho teach us about fear? Or about the power of confidence?
- How do we tell the difference between the kind of confidence that helps us win battles and the foolhardy confidence that can get us into trouble?
- If you believe God is calling you to take some action that seems illogical, how can you determine whether it's really the Lord speaking to you?
- Have you ever done something because you felt God was directing you to, even though most people would have told you to do something else? If so, how did things turn out?

Chapter 20

SAMSON: POWERED BY MULLET

(JUDGES 13–15)

With the Lord's help, the Israelites conquered much of the Promised Land. But after Joshua died, the Hebrew people began to disobey God. As you can read in the book of Judges, the Israelites began to follow a certain pattern: they would stray from following the Lord and would start worshiping idols. So God would punish them, allowing their enemies to overtake them and make their lives miserable. The Israelite people would finally wise up and cry to God for help. So God would send "judges," faithful men who would lead revolts against the enemies of the Israelites and remind the Jewish people to worship the one true God. That would lead to a period of peace and harmony. But then the Israelites would forget about God and start worshiping idols, and the cycle would start all over again.

One of the enemies of the Israelites was the Philistines. Their nation was near the Israelite homelands, and God often used them to punish his people. The Philistines were known for being mighty warriors and conquering many of the cities in the region. They also had a reputation for being uncultured, boorish, and uncouth; in other words, definitely not the high-society types.

Manoah was an Israelite living in Canaan during a period of Philistine rule. He was married, but the Bible doesn't tell us his wife's name. One day, an angel from God approached Manoah's wife, who was out in the fields, and said to her: "See now, you are barren and childless" (Judg. 13:3). This probably wasn't the best ice-breaker for a conversation with a woman who probably desperately wanted to have kids but was unable to. But this particular angel apparently wasn't blessed with the greatest people-skills. The conversation moved in a positive direction from there when he then told the woman she was going to have a son.

The angel explained to her that the boy's life would be dedicated to God and that, someday, he would help the Israelites be free from the Philistines. The angel then told her that, for her end of the bargain, she must never cut the boy's hair. She also couldn't drink wine or eat food that wasn't considered "clean" according to Moses' law.

When the baby was born, his parents named him Samson. He grew up to be big and strong but a bit of a wild-child. Much to his parents' disappointment, instead of marrying a nice Hebrew girl, Samson fell hard for a Philistine woman. His mom and dad tried to get him to reconsider his choice in life partners, but Samson would have none of it. He said to his dad, "Get her for me; for she pleases me well" (Judg. 14:3).

His parents didn't realize that Samson's ill-advised choice was part of God's plan to free the Israelites from the control of the Philistines. Manoah arranged for his son to meet the young lady, one thing led to another, and the two got married. Unfortunately, the marriage was doomed from the first day of the wedding feast.

Despite the enchanting power of young love, the power of hatred—at least between the Israelites and the Philistines—proved stronger. Samson didn't help matters much when he bet his thirty Philistine groomsmen that they could not answer his riddle: "Out of the eater came out food. Out of the strong came out sweetness" (Judg. 14:14).

Samson had made up the riddle after he killed a lion with his bare hands and then later found a swarm of bees making honey in the lion's carcass. He gave his groomsmen seven days to figure out the answer. The prize? Thirty sets of clothes and other garments. Although this seems like a strange jackpot, who knows? Maybe, despite being uncultured, boorish, and uncouth, the Philistines were budding fashionistas.

In any case, the Philistines took the bet but were stumped by the riddle. They secretly approached Samson's young wife and threatened to kill her and her father if she didn't get the riddle answer from her husband. So she cried, begged, pleaded, pouted, and finally coaxed the answer out of her newlywed husband. She then promptly told the Philistine groomsmen, who proudly announced the answer to Samson and told him to pay up.

Things went downhill really fast from that point. Samson realized the Philistines had cheated, so he went out and killed thirty Philistines, took their clothes, and paid the bet with them. The incident triggered a bunch of violent and deadly brawls between the Philistines and Samson.

Once, when he was seeking revenge for another embarrassment, Samson rounded up 300 foxes, tied their tails together in pairs, and attached torches to their tails. He then lit the torches and set the foxes free in the Philistines' grain fields and vineyards. As you might expect, the Philistines' entire harvest was burnt to a crisp. The Philistines took revenge on Samson by burning his wife and father-in-law to death.

Get the picture? Back in the ancient world, when people wanted to get revenge on their enemies, they didn't mess around. Although the Philistines kept trying to capture Samson, he kept getting the upper hand. Once, he killed a thousand of them with the jawbone of a donkey.

With God's help, Samson always managed to escape—that is, until he met the beautiful and treacherous Delilah ...

WHAT DO YOU THINK?

- In the Bible, the Lord often chose to bring special babies to couples who had not been able to have children. These babies often grew up to play large roles in God's plans. Why do you think God would choose these couples?
- The Philistines were the enemies of the Israelites, so why didn't Samson's parents stop him from marrying a Philistine woman?
- What can Samson's choices tell you about picking a spouse or close friend? Should we always follow our hearts? Or should we also consider a person's religious beliefs, values, and life's goals?

Chapter 21

MOMMA WARNED ME ABOUT GIRLS LIKE YOU

(JUDGES 16)

From before his birth, Samson had been blessed by God to be a mighty man, strong as an ox, and a hero to his people. Although he kept his lifelong vows to God, he was the kind of guy who lived life on his own terms. But he also had some major flaws. He didn't always think before he acted, which caused many problems for many people. And he had terrible taste in women.

Enter Delilah. She was no doubt a charmer, extremely beautiful, and clever as a fox. However, from what we know about her, she seemed like the type who would sell her own mother down the river for a pack of chewing gum—maybe even an already-chewed stick of gum. But Delilah's weak moral character didn't matter to Samson, who just couldn't resist her. As it turns out, she was the one enemy that he couldn't overcome.

When the Philistine leaders saw that Samson was spending a lot of time in Delilah's love nest, they approached her with a deal, offering her thousands of shekels of silver if she could pry out of Samson the secret to his incredible strength. That was a heck of a lot of money, considering Judas was paid only thirty shekels of silver for betraying Jesus. It was a deal she couldn't refuse. Delilah didn't know that Samson's strength came from his thick mane of hair that God had ordered to never be cut. But she planned on using her feminine wiles to get the secret out of him.

One night, when Delilah was being all lovey-dovey with Samson, she asked him about the secret to his strength. Samson, playing mind-games with his evil love interest, said if he were tied up with seven fresh green cords, he would lose all of his strength. Delilah wasted no time setting her trap for Samson.

The Philistines brought her some fresh green cords, and then hid in her house. When Samson fell asleep, she tied him up with seven of the cords and then yelled something to the effect of: "Oh no! Samson, look! Unbeknownst to little ol' me, the Philistines were hiding in my shoe closet and now are about to capture you in your unfortunate state of weakness. Woe is me, woe is me." Probably laughing that he out-tricked his deceitful girlfriend, Samson broke the green cords like a "thread is broken when it touches the fire" (Judg. 16:9) and tossed the Philistines out on their uncultured and boorish tushies.

Two more times, Delilah begged Samson to divulge the secret to his strength. And both times he gave her other phony explanations for how he could be made weak, like being bound with new ropes or having his hair braided into a weaving loom. And each time, she had the Philistines planted in her house, only to find that Samson, once again, was making a fool out of her.

You would think that Samson would have caught on that Delilah was doing everything in her power to help the Philistines rob him of his strength so they could capture and kill him. But Delilah kept at him. She begged, she nagged, she cried, she accused him of not loving her. And she did it day after day after day. Finally, the big lunkhead gave in.

"No razor has ever come on my head; for I have been a Nazirite to God from my mother's womb. If I am shaved, then my strength will go from me and I will become weak, and be like any other man," (Judg. 16:17) he told her.

Delilah knew that he was telling the truth this time, so she once again summoned the Philistines to come and hide out in her house. Delilah coaxed Samson to fall asleep with his head in her lap and then called the Philistines to give him the haircut of a lifetime. Samson awoke, saw the Philistines in Delilah's house, and prepared to give them one more shellacking—he didn't know that God had "departed from him" (Judg. 16:20). His muscles were as limp as an overcooked noodle. The Philistines jumped Samson, gouged out his eyes, and dragged him back to their city, where they threw him in prison.

Shortly thereafter, the Philistines were having a feast to pay homage to their fake god, Dagon, and were congratulating themselves for their victory over their archenemy, Samson. In the midst of their revelry, they decided to bring out poor, blind Samson and put him on display for public ridicule. What the Philistines didn't realize was that Samson's hair had started to grow back. They led Samson to the front of the temple and stood him between the two pillars that supported the weight of the entire building, which was filled with Philistine lords and ladies. Samson asked the boy who was guiding him to help him feel each of the two pillars with his hands so he could lean on them.

Then Samson reached out to God: "Lord … remember me, please, and strengthen me, please, only this once, God, that I may be at once avenged of the Philistines for my two eyes. ... Let me die with the Philistines!" (Judg. 16:28–30). With all of his might, Samson pushed on the two pillars and discovered that God had indeed restored his strength. The pillars, and the entire building, came crashing down. Along with Samson, over 3,000 Philistines died in that building collapse, more than Samson had previously killed in his entire life.

Even though Samson triumphs in the end, his story is also kind of sad. It underscores the enormous power that temptation can have over us. Samson's sin was jumping into relationships with the wrong women and letting his passion get so out-of-control that he lost all rationality and decency. In the early years, Samson had everything going for him: loving and devoted parents, God's blessing for his life, and his superpower strength. But his soft spot for the wrong ladies cost him just about everything.

Delilah had trouble written all over her from day one. But Samson let his obsession with her completely overpower him, even ignoring the obvious signs that she was trying to trap and destroy him. As we journey through life, we see people whose lives are ruined when they give in to powerful temptations like drugs, alcohol, gambling, greed, or uncontrollable and unhealthy physical attractions. Often, only prayer and a committed relationship with our Creator can help us muster the strength to escape the death-grip of these powerful sins.

But Samson also shows us that God does have a specific purpose in his master plan for each and every one of us. The Lord draws, not only from our unique talents and strengths, but sometimes also from our flaws. Samson's predisposition for making horrible relationship choices ushered him into a lifelong cage match with the Philistines that ultimately cost him his life. But it also helped him punish the people who were mistreating the Israelites, even in his last moments. God answered his impassioned plea and allowed him to end his life in glory while also taking a huge step toward ending the Philistines' rule over the Israelites. Samson will always be remembered for his brave sacrifice of his own life and final victory over his oppressors. His story should also be a reminder that even our flaws, weaknesses, and imperfections can find their way into God's plan for our lives, so long as we stay faithful to him.

WHAT DO YOU THINK?

- Sometimes our attraction to that special boy or girl can become a destructive obsession, almost like a drug addiction, that can cause us to lose all sense of reason. Do you think that's what was going on with Samson?
- Make a list of Samson's good and bad qualities. Now make a similar list for Moses. Are there qualities that make each man better suited for the job that God called him for?
- It is often obvious which behaviors could have devastating consequences to us or the people around us. So why do so many people engage in those harmful activities to begin with?
- What are some strategies you can deploy to resist particularly harmful temptations, such as drugs, alcohol, gambling, or a bad relationship?

Chapter 22

FRIENDS TO THE END

(RUTH 1–4)

The book of Ruth tells the story of a Hebrew woman named Naomi. She had a fairly happy existence until a horrible famine hit her country. Things got so bad for Naomi, her husband, and their two sons that they had to move away from their home near Bethlehem in Judah to the land of Moab. For a while, life got better there. They found food, and the two boys grew up and married Moabite women. Then Naomi's husband died. And then her sons died.

In that time and culture, life was hard for a woman with no husband or children to support her. Naomi's daughters-in-law, Orpah and Ruth, wanted to help out, but they too were widows without a lot going for them. Naomi decided she would return to her hometown in Judah, where she knew more people, including some of her relatives. Orpah and Ruth started out with Naomi.

But along the way, Naomi realized that she was taking her daughters-in-law away from *their* homelands and family. So she told them to turn around and go home. "You've been very good to me," she told them, "but you would be better off if you stayed home. Go back and find a new husband and may God bless you with children and a happy life."

Although she was sad to leave Naomi, Orpah saw the wisdom in her words and turned around. But Ruth didn't budge.

Don't urge me to leave you, and to return from following you, for where you go, I will go; and where you stay, I will stay. Your people will be my people, and your God my God. Where you die, I will die, and there I will be buried. (Ruth 1:16–17)

So Ruth returned with Naomi to her hometown and set to work getting food and supplies to care for her mother-in-law. Her selfless acts caught the attention of Boaz, one of the wealthier guys in town. He and Ruth got married and had a baby, but they never forgot about Naomi, and they all lived happily ever after.

The story of Ruth's incredible love and loyalty has inspired many people for thousands of years, including Metropolitan Kirill, an Eastern Orthodox bishop living in Bulgaria during World War II. At that time, the Nazis, led by Adolf Hitler, were committing horrible acts of cruelty, especially targeting the Jewish people. They rounded up millions of Jews in the countries they controlled and sent them to concentration camps to be systematically killed.

One night, the Nazi soldiers removed thousands of Jewish families from their homes in Bulgaria and packed them into a freight train destined for Treblinka, a horrific concentration camp in Poland where hundreds of thousands of people died. As the Nazis stood on the train platform ready to depart, a tall man wearing a flowing black robe emerged from the fog and darkness, leading 300 Christians from his church. It was Metropolitan Kirill. When Kirill reached the platform, he raised his arms and proclaimed he would not let the Nazis take the Jewish people away. He declared he would throw himself across the railroad tracks to stop the train from leaving the station.

He then turned to the people in the train and quoted the beautiful words Ruth had spoken to Naomi: "Where you go I will go, and where you stay I will stay. Your people will be my people and your God my God."

Kirill's actions stunned the Nazis and inspired other Bulgarians to join the effort to protect the country's Jews. The people on the train were eventually freed and allowed to return home, and Bulgaria allowed no mass extermination or relocation of its Jewish population during World War II.

In your journey here on earth, God may call upon you to perform an act of bravery to rescue another human being who desperately needs help. Reflecting on the models of unselfish love we see in the stories of Ruth and Bishop Kirill might help you muster the strength and courage you need when that moment arrives.

WHAT DO YOU THINK?

- Ruth and Metropolitan Kirill both took huge risks to stand by others in their hour of need. What might have inspired their extraordinary level of courage, self-sacrifice, and loyalty?
- Describe examples of other people who also stood by another human being, despite risks and sacrifices.
- Do you think it is significant that both Ruth and Metropolitan Kirill stood by people who were from different cultures and traditions?

Chapter 23

THE *BONK* HEARD 'ROUND THE WORLD

(1 SAMUEL 17)

The Bible story of David and Goliath is familiar to most people: little guy slays giant with just one rock to the head from his trusty sling. David, the little guy, is the same David who later became one of the most revered kings of Israel and author of many of the most beautifully written Psalms. Goliath, on the other hand, was neither revered nor eloquent; he was just big and ugly.

The Israelites and the Philistines were battling for control of Canaan. Goliath, the biggest, strongest, and fiercest of the Philistine warriors, daily taunted the Israelites, challenging them to send out their mightiest warrior to engage him in a one-on-one fight to the death. The prize? The winner's nation would be declared the victor of the war, and the loser's nation would become the winner's servants. But there were no warriors in the Israelite camp who wanted any part of that challenge. Until David showed up.

David was just the puny kid brother of some Israelite soldiers, but he convinced the ruler of Israel, King Saul, that God would give him the victory over Goliath. So the Israelites unexpectedly accepted the challenge and sent out David. Goliath was insulted when he saw some punk kid heading out for the death match.

He bellowed, "Come to me, and I will give your flesh to the birds of the sky, and to the animals of the field" (1 Sam. 17:44). Apparently, that was the ancient world's version of trash-talking. David responded with a little trash-talking of his own.

> You come to me with a sword, with a spear, and with a javelin; but I come to you in the name of … the God of the armies of Israel. … Today, Yahweh will deliver you into my hand. I will strike you and take your head from off you … that all the earth may know that there is a God in Israel and that all this assembly may know that Yahweh doesn't save with sword and spear; for the battle is Yahweh's, and he will give you into our hand (1 Sam. 17:45–47).

Then David launched a rock from his sling that bonked Goliath right in the head. Down went the giant, face first, crashing to the ground. As it turns out, contrary to what Goliath had said, it wasn't David's flesh that became bird food that day.

David's incredible faith in God enabled him to do the impossible. The Bible gives us many details about David and how he lived his life. And one fact shines through each and every story: David turned his life over to God at an early age and remained true to the Lord, despite all the obstacles the world threw his way. David was not perfect. He stumbled and sinned in his lifetime, but he always returned to God, putting aside his own agenda and surrendering himself to our Creator.

The fight with Goliath demonstrates how David's decision to live according to God's will enabled him to accept any challenge without fearing the outcome. David even refused to wear armor or carry a sword into battle. He knew God would protect him.

God offers that same confidence and peace of mind to each and every one of us. Surrender your life to God and be obedient to him, and, like David, you can accomplish the impossible without worrying what the future might bring. On the other hand, people who reject God in order to satisfy their own wants and desires are teetering on a tightrope without a safety net. Even if it seems for a while that they're living the good life, sooner or later, a life without God feels empty and lacking true happiness or meaning.

It all comes down to a choice. Either choose a life separate from God, which comes with the worry that things can fall apart at any moment, or follow the Lord and enjoy extraordinary confidence in knowing you can achieve greatness and will have the happiest of endings.

WHAT DO YOU THINK?

- David's extraordinary bravery and confidence came from his decision to surrender his life to God. Surrendering your life to someone else—even to the Lord—can sound pretty scary. What are the real fears and other obstacles that often stop people from taking this step?
- Goliath had his own brand of confidence, which caused him to underestimate David. How would you describe the differences between David's form of confidence and Goliath's?
- What types of things could you accomplish if you truly believed, with all your heart, that God would protect you and stand by you no matter what? What "Goliaths" in your life could God help you defeat?

Chapter 24

WILL THE REAL "BAD MOMMY" PLEASE STAND UP?

(1 KINGS 3)

David's battle with Goliath was just the first step in his long history of service to the Israelite nation. He was a mighty warrior, a beloved king, a poet, a musician. He served as a military commander for King Saul and then spent years of his life running from Saul, who was trying to kill him out of jealousy. After Saul died, David became king and reigned over Israel for forty years. Some of the most amazing stories in the Bible are about David's life; read about them in the books of First and Second Samuel. You can also read many of David's beautiful poems in the book of Psalms.

Toward the end of his life, David passed the royal torch to Solomon, his son with Bathsheba. Solomon was only a teenager when he became king.

One night, not long after Solomon had become king, the Lord appeared to Solomon in a dream and asked what divine gift he wanted. Solomon confessed that he barely had a clue about ruling an entire kingdom so asked the Lord for wisdom. He wanted to be a good judge of what's right and what's wrong, who is good and who isn't. God was impressed that Solomon didn't make one of the typical requests, like piles of money, a long life, or for God to squash his enemies. So the Lord granted Solomon his wish—and then some, telling Solomon:

> *Behold, I have given you a wise and understanding heart; so that there has been no one like you before you, and after you none will arise like you. I have also given you that which you have not asked, both riches and honor, so that there will not be any among the kings like you for all your days (1 Kings 3:12–13).*

Solomon got to show off his infinite wisdom when two women brought him a baby and a sad story. Woman 1 explained that she and Woman 2 lived together in the same house. Both had given birth to baby boys at the same time. Woman 1 said Woman 2 had accidentally rolled over on her baby in bed, suffocating him. According to Woman 1, Woman 2 then sneaked into her room and swapped the lifeless body of her own baby for Woman 1's baby.

Woman 2 agreed with this account of what happened except for one important detail: she argued that it was Woman 1 who accidentally killed her baby and was lying about which mother stole the other's child. Just in case you've lost track, both women were claiming the live baby boy as their own.

Solomon recognized that this was going to be a tough situation to resolve since there were no witnesses to any of this. After pondering what to do and who to believe, he announced his decision. He asked his servant to bring a sword and to cut the living baby right down the middle so he could give half of the baby to each of the women. Share-share, that's fair, right?

Just when the sword was about to cut through the baby boy, one of the women cried out to Solomon to stop this insanity. "Give her the baby," she cried. "Don't kill him!" The other woman, we'll call her Evil-Baby-Thief, seemed fine with receiving her one-half of the baby. King Solomon then stopped the proceedings and told his servants to give the baby to the woman who had been ready to surrender him. "Give her the living child, and definitely do not kill him. She is his mother" (1 Kings 3:27). King Solomon knew that the real mother would rather give up her own baby than to watch it be killed.

This story cemented King Solomon's reputation for extraordinary wisdom. But the real hero in this story was the mother who demonstrated the depth of her love for her child. This woman was put into the terrible position of having to instantly decide between two horrific choices: a) let Evil-Baby-Thief take her son, knowing the child would be raised by a liar and a crook who also was negligent enough to have killed her own baby; or b) sit back and watch her son be cut in half. Laying down your life for your child is an act of love most parents would be willing to do in a heartbeat. But agreeing to hand your baby over to your enemy? Well, that's probably one of the most painful sacrifices anyone could ever imagine.

In some ways, the good mother in this story represents our Father in Heaven, who has to make a similar sacrifice every time a new baby is born. God releases each of us, his children, into a harsh world that is under the power of Satan. (See 1 John 5:19.) Why does God hand us over into a place where sin and temptation reign and where no person is spared a healthy dose of suffering? Why doesn't God just keep us bubble-wrapped in a place that is safe and always happy, like the Garden of Eden, where all of our needs are met and where pain, sadness, and life's inevitable disappointments simply don't exist?

God sends us into the real world because that is the only way we become strong, wise, and fully formed adults, who come to God by choice, not because we have no other option. Our Heavenly Father is willing to endure the heartbreak of sitting by and watching his children suffer sickness, physical pain, the loss of loved ones, and feelings of loneliness, rejection, or personal failure.

Like the real mother in the story of wise old King Solomon, God is willing to give us up and send us out in our world where the Enemy reigns. And he does it because he loves us so much that he wants each of us to have a shot at life, a real life, that has true meaning and purpose, and can continue for all eternity.

WHAT DO YOU THINK?

- The real mother loved her baby so much that she would give it up to be raised by a bad person in order to save the child's life. Do you know anyone who has surrendered control over someone they love to save them from some unfortunate fate?
- What is the difference between being "smart" and having "wisdom"? If you had a choice of being super-smart or super-wise, which would you pick? Why?
- Do you believe there is one set of truths in the universe or do you believe there could be many? If there can only be one set of truths, how will you find out what it is?
- What would you say to those who argue: "People can have different views on the truth and they all can be right"?

Chapter 25

THE STORY OF JOB: AND YOU THOUGHT *YOU* HAD A BAD DAY

(JOB 1–42)

The Bible has a lot to say about how God wants us to live our lives, treat one another, and connect with him. He makes it clear that he loves each and every one of us and can use whatever comes our way to help us grow closer to him and become better people. However, the Bible tells us little, if anything, about God's thought processes or why he lets certain things happen here on earth. The only thing we know for sure is that God REALLY hates it when we presume to know what he's thinking. We learn that in the book of Job, which tells us about a wealthy man who loved God.

Job had it all: wealth, a beautiful family, lots of kids, and the respect of his entire community. But in a matter of days, everything was taken away from him. His losses piled up so fast that everybody just assumed that Job had done something really horrible to infuriate God. Job knew that was not true, but he had no idea why he suddenly became the target of so much misery.

As readers, we get a better idea of what's going on because the book of Job opens with God and Satan having a conversation. Satan told God that he had been traveling around the earth, no doubt looking for vulnerable souls to snatch for his army of evildoers. Probably wanting to give the Devil a little poke, God asked if he had come across Job, describing him as "a blameless and an upright man, one who fears God, and turns away from evil" (Job 1:8).

"Yeah, I've seen him," Satan replied. "No surprise that he's *sooo* good—you've given him the perfect life. He has ten beautiful kids, plenty of wealth, herds of livestock, servants galore, and land as far as the eye could see." Satan told God that Job wouldn't be so righteous if he didn't have such a cushy life.

God was confident in Job's heart, so he gave the Devil permission to strip away from Job whatever he wanted so that God could prove that Job's faith was deeper than his success. But God placed one condition on the Devil: he could not physically harm Job. Satan wasted no time sticking it to poor Job.

All in one day, Job lost everything. A group of bandits attacked and killed many of his servants and stole all of his oxen and many of his camels. A firestorm burned all of Job's sheep and killed even more servants. Another group of robbers invaded Job's property, stole the remaining camels, and killed nearly every remaining servant. Finally, a violent windstorm destroyed the house where Job's children were celebrating, killing every single one of them. After losing just about everything and everyone in his life, Job stayed true to God, saying: "Naked I came out of my mother's womb, and naked will I return there. Yahweh gave, and Yahweh has taken away. Blessed be Yahweh's name" (Job 1:21).

Not too much later, God met up with the Devil again and gave him a big "I-told-you-so." Despite losing everything, Job had not turned on the Lord. The Devil claimed he wasn't impressed. "Sure, Job didn't curse you. That's because I just took away things and people. Let me take away his health and give him physical pain and he'll turn on you like a rattlesnake."

"All right," God said. "You can make him hurt. But you can't kill him."

So Satan struck Job with a horrible skin disease, covering him from head to toe in painful sores. More and more of Job's friends—and even his wife—became convinced that Job had done something horrible to deserve such punishment. "Why don't you just curse God and die?" she asked him. But Job was steadfast in not blaming God for his troubles, asking, "Should we worship God only when things are going our way?"

Although Job was saying the right things, he was suffering and miserable. Three of his buddies, Eliphaz, Bildad, and Zophar, heard about Job's tragedies and showed up to comfort him. But they barely recognized him, with all of his festering sores, looking like a pile of raw hamburger meat, and they sobbed at the sight of him. Then they sat on the ground with him in total silence for seven days and seven nights, just sharing in his grief and offering their silent support.

After seven days, Job began to speak. He cried out in his agony that his life had turned into an utter train wreck and he wished he had never been born. His friends then decided it was time for them to offer Job their "wisdom" and advice. The three men took turns explaining that since God is fair and just, he wouldn't allow someone to suffer so much unless they truly deserved to be punished. Therefore, Job must have done something horrible to deserve all his suffering. Eliphaz said to Job: "Isn't your wickedness great? ... For you have ... stripped the naked of their clothing. You haven't given water to the weary to drink, and you have withheld bread from the hungry. ... You have sent widows away empty ... Therefore snares are around you" (Job 22:5–10).

But Job was having none of it. He kept arguing that he was innocent, that he had done *nothing* to deserve this punishment. In fact, Job believed that God owed him an explanation for why he was treating his faithful servant so badly. He wanted God to show up and answer for his actions. Eventually, Job's three friends realized they were wasting their breath because Job was never going to agree with them.

Then, a younger man named Elihu entered the conversation. First, he scolded Job's friends for not having good answers to Job's complaints about the Lord. He then told Job that he was wrong for saying the Lord just sits by and doesn't answer when we cry out to him when suffering. God does respond, Elihu said, but the communication is often subtle, coming through thoughts or dreams. Sometimes we miss the message because we're just not listening.

But Elihu also had some different ideas about why God sometimes lets bad things happen to us. Bad things aren't always a punishment, Elihu said. In fact, he believed that God can use hardships to transform us into better versions of ourselves. In the same way that iron is put into a fiery furnace to purify, strengthen, and turn it into steel, God can use life's experiences, which are sometimes very painful, to make us stronger, wiser, and more loving souls. And when we let pride, self-indulgence, or arrogance overtake our lives, Elihu reasoned, adversity can sometimes rescue us from the devastating consequences of sin by giving us a wake-up call to get our lives back on track.

OUT OF THE WHIRLWIND

These five men had been sitting around arguing with each other for days, when suddenly God spoke. In all of his awe and majesty, the Lord answered Job "out of the whirlwind" (Job 38:1). Job must have been terrified when the Lord said to him, "Brace yourself like a man, for I will question you, then you answer me!" (Job 38:3).

Job had been demanding for days that God show up so he could ask him questions about why he was suffering so much. Now God, the creator of the universe, *had* shown up, but he wasn't answering any questions—he was asking them.

God's first question was a doozy. "Where were you when I laid the foundations of the earth?" (Job 38:4). Who measured the earth and decided how big it would be? Who poured the foundation or started the construction? Basically, the Lord was saying, "Job, you think you're so important and you know so much, but there are a lot of really basic questions you can't even begin to answer."

And God didn't stop there; he just kept firing questions at Job. Can you command the morning and the night, the lightning and the rain, the winds, the hail, and the snow? Have you ever walked in the depths of the seas or stood at the gates of death? Did you create every creature that ever lived? "Is it by your wisdom that the hawk soars" or "at your command that the eagle mounts up, and makes his nest on high?" (Job 39:26–27).

Finally, Job got his chance to speak, and he seemed to have forgotten that he had some questions for God.

I know that you can do all things, and that no purpose of yours can be restrained ... therefore I have uttered that which I didn't understand, things too wonderful for me, which I didn't know. ... I had heard of you by the hearing of the ear, but now my eye sees you. Therefore I abhor myself, and repent in dust and ashes (Job 42:2–6).

Job never did ask God all the questions he wanted to ask, and it appears that God never offered Job an explanation for his suffering. In the presence of God, Job and his friends realized all their combined wisdom was a speck of dust when compared to the Lord's power, wisdom, and majesty. Job stopped trying to blame God for his misery, and his friends realized they didn't know much about it either. The Lord had especially harsh words for Eliphaz, Bildad, and Zophar. He scolded them for self-righteously condemning Job and telling him his fate was the result of some terrible sin. Turns out, they didn't have any justification for their accusations.

When you suffer, do you blame God for your pain? When you see someone else suffering, do you question why God would let that happen? God's interaction with Job demonstrates that we shouldn't fool ourselves into thinking we have any standing to criticize or question the Lord Almighty.

And God's rebuke of Eliphaz, Bildad, and Zophar should make us very skeptical of people who pretend to have special insight into God's thinking, especially when they judge someone who is dealing with a personal tragedy. It can be hard to accept that the Lord can be loving, kind, and just and still allow bad things to happen to good people. But the story of Job teaches us that a good person can indeed suffer terrible hardships.

Job shows us clearly that we cannot pretend to know the

mind of God—especially when it comes to suffering. All we can know for sure is that God is mighty and wise and powerful beyond our wildest imaginations and that his love for us is limitless. If we remain faithful to him, whatever happens to us here on earth is ultimately for our good and will somehow fit into God's plan. Beyond that, we have to accept that there is much that we'll never understand, at least in this lifetime.

As for our friend Job, his life's story did have a happy ending. After he repented for demanding that God justify himself, the Lord forgave him. And then God blessed Job by giving him "twice as much as he had before" and allowing him to live a rich and full life to a very old age (Job 42:12–17).

WHAT DO YOU THINK?

- Have you ever felt like Job? Like everything in your life is going bad and there is no limit to the pain that you're suffering? Did you reach out to God for help? How did things turn out?
- The reaction of Job's friends is fairly common, unfortunately. People often find some reason to blame the person who is suffering because they don't like to believe that bad things sometimes happen to good people. Have you seen people you know who acted like Job's friends?
- God can reward us when we're obedient and can impose consequences when we're not. But unpleasant things can happen even when we are abiding by the Lord's plans for our life. How can we reconcile those two realities?
- Have you ever questioned God's actions or challenged his reasons for doing something in your life? What does the book of Job say about that?

Chapter 26

THE ORIGINAL *SOUL* MUSIC (LONG BEFORE MOTOWN)

(PSALMS 1–150)

Next time you're ready to torque up your Spotify playlist, consider pulling out the book of Psalms instead. I know that sounds so dorky—only a dad (or a youth pastor) would even have the gall to suggest that. But hear me out!

The Psalms are God's version of a great rock or rap song. They have amazing lyrics and were intended to be sung. And if you release yourself into whatever emotions a particular Psalm ignites, you just might find yourself transcended to another place.

When you read the Psalms, it's best not to overanalyze the verses bit by bit in an attempt to uncover some hidden meaning in each line or phrase. In fact, if you do, the meaning might fall apart and you'll miss the point entirely. You'll definitely get the most out of these chapters if you just let the rhythm of the verses wash over you and enjoy the vivid imagery and emotions created by the poetry. Like a great song, a great Psalm won't lose its impact over time but will get better with each reading.

The individual Psalms fall into several categories. Many are songs of praise for God's magnificent glory and his creation of our awesome universe. Others are expressions of thanksgiving for his wonderful blessings. Some are Psalms of lament—mourning hardships and suffering and pain. Several provide words of wisdom or guidance on matters of the spirit.

The Psalms were written by multiple authors and were composed over several centuries. However, they share one common element: all paint a vivid and mighty image of a loving and all-powerful God who is the one true source of our hope for the future, our joy, and our very existence.

One of the most, if not *the* most, cherished chapters in all the Bible is Psalm 23. While Psalm 23 can evoke different feelings for different people, in my life, it's been the perfect antidote for those days when I felt scared, beaten-down, or alone. You've probably heard it a million times, but it's worth reading it again here.

[The Lord] is my shepherd:
I shall lack nothing.
He makes me lie down in green pastures.
He leads me beside still waters.
He makes my soul be free.
He guides me in the paths of righteousness for his name's sake.
Even though I walk through the valley of the shadow of death,
I will fear no evil, for you are with me.
Your rod and your staff, they comfort me.
You prepare a table before me in the presence of my enemies.
You anoint my head with oil.
My cup runs over.

Surely goodness and loving kindness shall follow me all the
days of my life,
and I will dwell in [the Lord's] house forever.

Reading Psalm 23 always leaves me feeling safe, secure, and at peace: the way I used to feel when I was little and would sit at the kitchen table while my mom made dinner. Or when I'd crawl into bed with my parents after having a bad dream. It also gives me the courage to move forward in my journey here on earth with strength and purpose. This Psalm reminds me that, so long as I stay by God's side, he will keep me out of harm's way and carry me through life's most difficult challenges.

Other Psalms might speak to you and become your own source of inspiration. Much depends on where you are in your own life's journey. But you won't know until you poke around this wonderful book of the Old Testament; it's definitely worth checking out.

WHAT DO YOU THINK?

- When you listen to your favorite songs, do you always listen closely to the lyrics?
- What do you think makes a song really great: the lyrics, the melody, the rhythm?
- Do you have a favorite Psalm? If so, is it a praise to God, a thanksgiving, a lament, or a wisdom Psalm?
- How does Psalm 23 make you feel?

Chapter 27

THE LORD'S WISDOM, IN TASTY BITE-SIZED PIECES

(PROVERBS 1–31)

When it comes to selecting ice cream, you probably pick the flavor that best fits your mood. Had an awesome day? Might be time for a scoop of cotton candy ice cream on a sugar cone covered in rainbow sprinkles. Failed an algebra test and dropped your phone in the bathtub? Might be the day for a double-chocolate dip of dark chocolate fudge.

Similarly, at the end of a long day when you're ready to curl up with your Bible, you can select a reading that satisfies your spiritual craving *du jour*. Feeling deep and wanting to ponder the meaning of life? Go to Ecclesiastes. Feeling like life just kicked you in the teeth? Read about Job and commiserate with him over his catastrophic misfortunes while wallowing in your own self-pity-party. If the book of Job were an item on the ice-cream shop menu, it would be a jumbo death-by-chocolate sundae, extra hot fudge, hold the whipped cream.

And then there's the book of Proverbs. It's perfect when you're in the mood for some individually packaged jewels of wisdom to help you navigate life's choppy waters. Proverbs gets right to the point with little bites of practical advice that you can appreciate on days when you just don't have the time or energy to dive into more complicated Bible stories, parables, or prophecies. In other words, Proverbs can give you a quick return on your investment of devotional reading time.

Being a Bible nerd, I have my own Top 15 Proverbs, which I have listed below with a short explanation of what each means to me. My favorites don't contain earth-shattering revelations on the deep dark secrets of the universe—they're just pearls of wisdom and common sense. Nevertheless, these proverbs help remind us of how to live in a way that's pleasing to God while succeeding in a world that can be quite difficult.

MY TOP 15 PROVERBS

1. "Whoever loves correction loves knowledge, but he who hates reproof is stupid." (Proverbs 12:1)

Yes, some people try to give you "constructive criticism" or "correction" that they're really offering so they can air their grievances against you—often, not very helpful. But this verse is talking about true Christian guidance, the kind of correction that is offered from a place of love and concern for you. Be sure to listen to this sort of feedback and use it as an opportunity to mature, gain insight into yourself, and become a better person. Anyone who is too proud to accept constructive advice delivered in love is just being "stupid."

2. **"The hands of the diligent ones shall rule, but laziness ends in slave labor."** (Proverbs 12:24)

Anything worthwhile in this world requires some measure of diligence, commitment, and hard work. There are no shortcuts to achieving good grades, making great friends, becoming a top athlete, or developing a deep relationship with God. If you think you can take the easy way out but still reach your goals, you're lying to yourself. As this proverb suggests, those who work hard most often become the successful leaders who run the show, while the lazy people remain at the bottom of the heap.

3. **"He who guards his mouth guards his soul. One who opens wide his lips comes to ruin."** (Proverbs 13:3)

Far too often, we get into trouble not because of our *actions* but because of our *words*. Think before you speak and choose your words carefully. People who use foul language, gossip, enjoy saying hurtful things, or just blather mindless nonsense all day will suffer the consequences, both spiritually and otherwise.

4. **"Poverty and shame come to him who refuses discipline, but he who heeds correction shall be honored."** (Proverbs 13:8)

Those who rebel against anyone in authority and refuse to accept the consequences for behaving badly never quite develop or mature. They continue to behave like bratty children even when they are adults. These people often lead unfulfilled lives and will forever live with bitterness and regret. But those who own their mistakes, accept responsibility for their actions, and vow to do better in the future develop into respected and successful women and men who lead meaningful and honorable lives.

5. **"One who walks with wise men grows wise, but a companion of fools suffers harm."** (Proverbs 13:20)

As social creatures, we humans cannot help being influenced by the people we hang out with—especially our closest family and friends. If you surround yourself with deadbeats, druggies, or just plain nasty people, you'll likely become one yourself; it's just human nature. But if you spend your time with people who are caring, conscientious, and responsible, they will rub off on you. And they will influence who you are and who you will be. Seek out friends, teammates, and role models who are kind, insightful, hard-working, and, most importantly, living according to God's Word.

6. **"A gentle answer turns away wrath, but a harsh word stirs up anger."** (Proverbs 15:1)

When someone is angry at you, don't throw gasoline on the fire by matching their aggression. Letting yourself wallow in your own fury and engage in an angry screaming fight or a flaming social media exchange is a lot like scratching an itchy rash. It feels so good, in a fiery kind of way, but is hard to stop once you get going. And even while you're scratching, or raging, you know you're going to regret it in the end. It's much better to stay calm, use kind words, and try to defuse the situation by rising above it. That way, you can extinguish the other person's anger and establish yourself as the grown-up in the room.

7. "All the ways of a man are clean in his own eyes; but [God] weighs the motives." (Proverbs 16:2)

Our brains are wired to make us believe we have good reasons for our bad thoughts, hurtful words, and harmful actions. We all want to see ourselves in a positive light— no matter how horribly we have behaved. That tendency to give ourselves a pass for any of our missteps makes it vitally important to touch base with God daily for a reality check. Pray, study your Bible, attend church, and hang out with other Christians. These channels help us stay in touch with our Creator so we can measure our intentions and behavior honestly. Seeing ourselves as God sees us can help us realize when we have a problem, fix what's broken, develop as Christians, and become better people.

8. "Before destruction the heart of man is proud, but before honor is humility." (Proverbs 18:12)

Pride takes two forms. First, there's the kind of pride you have when you or someone you care about accomplishes something great. I feel incredibly proud of my kids when I see them do something kind for someone or achieve a worthy goal. God favors this type of pride. But he despises the self-centered, boastful kind of pride referenced in this proverb. This damaging form of pride often is expressed through self-promotion, worldly ambition, and unhealthy competition. And, as the proverb suggests, this form of pride leads to destruction. If you want to live an honorable life and earn the respect of the people you care about, put aside any feelings of selfish pride and practice humility and service to others, just as our Lord Jesus did.

9. "Discipline your son, for there is hope; don't be a willing party to his death." (Proverbs 19:18)

Parents who truly love their children discipline them. It's the only way kids learn right from wrong, so that they can someday develop into responsible adults. The parents who let their kids do whatever they want and impose no boundaries may think they are making their children happy. But kids who grow up without learning self-discipline or how to work for what they want may never reach their true potential or even be fully functional grown-ups. Like any loving parent, our Heavenly Father disciplines us because he wants what is best for us.

10. "Whoever stops his ears at the cry of the poor, he will also cry out, but shall not be heard." (Proverbs 21:13)

It's easy for us to close our eyes and ears to the pain and hardship of those in need by convincing ourselves that some other kind person, one who isn't quite so busy or who has more money in the bank, will come to the rescue. However, as Christians, we all are called upon to answer the cries of the poor, the sick, and the vulnerable. At some point in our lives, we too will suffer and need the help of others. But if we live selfishly and never do a kind deed for anyone else, we might just find our own cries for help go unanswered.

11. "A good name is more desirable than great riches, and loving favor is better than silver and gold."

(Proverbs 22:1)

It's a worn-out cliché, but it's true: money can't buy happiness. Of course, living in poverty isn't much fun either, but we can be sure that the Lord will provide for all of our basic needs, so we shouldn't obsess over money. True happiness comes from being right with our Creator, enjoying relationships with our family and friends, and living honorable lives that have purpose and meaning. All of the money in the world can't buy those things that are the ultimate source of true and lasting joy, comfort, and fulfillment.

12. "Don't be among ones drinking too much wine, or those who gorge themselves on meat; for the drunkard and the glutton shall become poor; and drowsiness clothes them in rags." (Proverbs 23:20–21)

God wants us to enjoy the many things that he put here on earth for our pleasure, like good food, art, music, the company of good friends, the beauty of nature. But the people who *overindulge* in earthly pleasures, particularly the things that we put in our bodies, often end up suffering dire consequences, both physically and spiritually. We need to be careful about partaking in pleasures of the flesh, and completely resist those that have addictive qualities. Once you find yourself on that train heading down the tracks to self-destruction, it can be very difficult to jump off. It's better not to start.

13. "A wise man has great power. A knowledgeable man increases strength ..." (Proverbs 24:5)

It's funny that many kids, and even some adults, think being smart is uncool. But knowledge, intelligence, wisdom—whatever you want to call it—doesn't stop you from also being strong, bold, funny, the life of the party, or whatever you think is "cool." As this proverb suggests, having intelligence and know-how actually gives you power, freedom, and effectiveness in most situations. Of course, being smart isn't going to guarantee your happiness or your faithfulness to God's plan for your life. But obtaining wisdom will help you understand how the world works, which is an important building block for maturing, becoming a valuable contributor in society, and developing as a Christian. We should all strive to become as wise and knowledgeable as we can; there simply is no downside.

14. "Let another man praise you, and not your own mouth; a stranger, and not your own lips." (Proverbs 27:2)

Bragging doesn't make other people think you're wonderful. It only makes you look insecure, arrogant, or some combination of the two. Even subtle boasting that you try to pass off as a joke won't fool anyone. If you're good at what you do, people will take notice. Leave it to others to compliment or praise you. Boasting about our virtues or accomplishments just makes us look full of ourselves and kind of pathetic.

15. "One who works his land will have an abundance of food; but one who chases fantasies will have his fill of poverty."
(Proverbs 28:19)

Sometimes when I'm in the checkout line at the local convenience store, I become sad when the person in front of me, who looks like they need a shower and a hot meal, is buying lottery tickets. As we all know, you're more likely to get hit by lightning than win the mega-millions jackpot. But too many people squander their lives chasing fantasies and get-rich-quick schemes, like winning the lottery or playing in the NBA or becoming the next social media star. That is not to say that you shouldn't pursue your passion—the most successful people in this world have done just that. Just remember to incorporate your passion into a realistic career or life plan that includes achievable goals, periodic assessment of your progress toward those goals, and consistent hard work.

THE ODDBALL PROVERBS

When you really dig into the book of Proverbs, you're going to find some that are so oddly worded that they'll make you laugh, or cringe, or at least wonder if something got lost in the translation. But the Good Lord has his purpose for each and every one of them, even if it just takes a little extra reflection to figure out what the heck they're trying to say. I told you at the beginning of this chapter that I'm a Bible nerd—in fact, so much so that, in addition to having a Top 15 Proverbs list, I also have a Top 5 Oddball Proverbs list. And I'm willing to share:

1. **"Better is a dinner of herbs, where love is, than a fattened calf with hatred."** (Proverbs 15:17)
   I'm not sure which of the two would be less appetizing: a plate of herbs or a fatty piece of meat. But I get the point: a simple meal with people I love is better than a fancy party filled with people who are bitter and hateful.

2. **"One who winks his eyes to plot perversities, one who compresses his lips, is bent on evil."** (Proverbs 16:30)
   I've never paid too much attention to my own facial expressions. But apparently, in the interest of my spiritual well-being, I had better start. And if I've been going around compressing my lips, I better knock it off right away.

3. **"The sluggard buries his hand in the dish; he will not so much as bring it to his mouth again."** (Proverbs 19:24)
   Can you imagine being so lazy that you don't even bother using a spoon or fork? You just dip your hand into a bowl of food. And if you're *really* lazy, you just leave it there because it's too much work to shovel the food into your mouth. I hope that my loved ones would stage a serious intervention if I ever got to this point!

4. **"Have you found honey? Eat as much as is sufficient for you, lest you eat too much, and vomit it."** (Proverbs 25:16)
   You'd have to eat an awful lot of honey before it would make you vomit. My sense is, this is just a dramatic way of saying that even good things, if taken to excess, can be harmful.

5. "If your enemy is hungry, give him food to eat. If he is thirsty, give him water to drink; for you will heap coals of fire on his head, and [God] will reward you."

(Proverbs 25:21–22)

Maybe it's just me, but this one seems a bit harsh. Remind me never to accept a dinner invitation from the guy who wrote this one. But I think we're supposed to be paying attention to the kindness part, not the "fire-on-his-head" part. In other words, be kind to everyone—even to your enemies—and let God reward you for your deeds. And it's the Lord's job, not yours, to figure out whatever punishment the other guy deserves (like a head-full of burning coals!)

One final thought on Proverbs: my lists just touch the surface of the gems you can find there. Go explore this book for yourself and you will uncover a treasure trove of valuable insights and thoughtful wisdom, just there for the taking.

WHAT DO YOU THINK?

- Which one of my Top 15 Proverbs speaks to you the most and why?
- Look at the book of Proverbs and choose one or two Proverbs that are not in my Top 15. Why do you think your choices deserve special attention?
- What meaning can you find in my list of Oddballs that I may have missed?
- What do you like about receiving the Lord's guidance in bite-sized pieces, as you do in Proverbs? Are there times when Proverbs might not offer you the spiritual nourishment you need?

Chapter 28

THE WORLD'S GRAND DECEPTION: IF ONLY I COULD ... [FILL IN THE BLANK]

(ECCLESIASTES 1–12)

As high school students go, Allison is a rock star. Everyone knows that kid is goin' places. She has a 4.0 average, is president of her class, and heads the student mentor program in her town. She is about to sit for the SATs and is praying that she scores at least a 1,500. All Allison has ever wanted is to follow in her family's footsteps and attend Harvard. Her mother has told her many stories about all the wonderful traditions that make Harvard a one-of-a-kind place, and Allison knows that Harvard will give her a leg-up in landing her dream job as an investment banker in New York. Plus, she would be able to tell people for the rest of her life that she had attended this most prestigious university. The morning of the SAT, Allison prayed harder than she ever had in her life: "God, please help me ace the SAT. The only thing standing between me and total happiness is this stupid test!"

Jeremy is the star forward and top scorer on his high school basketball team. From the time that he was old enough to hold a basketball, he has spent nearly every waking hour on the court practicing his jump shot, working on his ball-handling skills, and playing in any game he could find. Recruiters from both North Carolina and Duke have contacted him, and he knows that either school would be a springboard toward his lifelong dream of playing in the NBA. He understands that very few basketball players make it to the NBA, but he believes that if he keeps giving 100 percent of himself to reaching his goal, he will someday make it in the big leagues, which he is sure will make his life complete.

Emma, a freshman in college, is right in the middle of sorority rush. She's been accepting invitations from several sororities, even though the parties, luncheons, and other social functions take time away from her studies. She is expecting to get bids from one or two of the sororities. But what she really wants is a bid from Gamma Phi Beta, the most popular sorority on campus. You see, when Emma was in high school, she had a nice group of friends, but they were a bit nerdy and definitely not the "It girls." Now that Emma is in college, she feels she can reinvent herself, and nothing would make her college years more spectacular than to become a sister at Gamma Phi, so she could finally be part of the cool crowd.

Whether it's acceptance to an Ivy League college, playing in the NBA, or joining the most popular sorority on campus, Allison, Jeremy, and Emma believe they know the secret to happiness and fulfillment here on earth. And adults are no different: "Lord, if I can just land this job, my money problems will be solved and we'll finally be able to feel secure and enjoy life." Or: "God, if I can just find the right partner, I can get married, have kids, and, no matter what else happens in my life, I'll be happy."

That's what the author of Ecclesiastes thought too. Until he got it all, did it all, tried it all, and found everything "meaningless."

The book of Ecclesiastes tackles the age-old question: "What is the meaning of life?" The author of this book doesn't give us his name, but he identifies himself in the first verse as "the Preacher, the son of David, king in Jerusalem." Based on that and other facts, many biblical scholars believe this book was written by wise old King Solomon. ("Ecclesiastes" is just another way of translating the Hebrew word that many of our English Bibles translate as "preacher.")

The author of this book, the Preacher, says he had been on a quest to determine what gives life true and lasting meaning. He didn't just ponder that question from his throne inside his fancy palace. Instead, he embarked on a lifelong journey that included a lot of trial and error to figure out what would give his life purpose, joy, and meaning.

Like many of us, the Preacher tried to find meaning in life by throwing himself into his work. He poured himself into creating spectacular estates and beautiful gardens, parks, and vineyards. He also acquired flocks and herds of all kinds of animals. As a result of his hard work, he amassed huge wealth, including gold, silver, and other treasures. But, after all of his efforts, the author realized that none of his worldly accomplishments brought him any lasting joy or meaning. It was like "chasing after the wind," he said (Eccl. 1:16).

Then he experimented with a completely different path: indulging in any and every pleasure that the world had to offer. The Preacher doesn't describe it all in detail, but he mentions wine and music, so we have to believe he was doing some pretty hard partying. But worldly pleasures didn't satisfy him or make him happy either. He said it was just more chasing after the wind.

So he tried gaining wisdom, studying all of the ancient texts, scholarly writings, and anything else he could get his hands on that would give him deep knowledge of how the world works. Eventually, he decided that being intelligent and having worldly insights is helpful, but it offers no lasting value or meaning.

After pursuing every avenue imaginable to achieve lasting happiness, the Preacher concluded that none of these worldly pursuits brought him real joy or fulfillment. They were all just distractions that took him away from the one thing that does bring true meaning to our lives: our connection to God. Only by living in the Lord's glorious light can we get that taste of heaven, that oasis of tranquility while we're still here on earth amid life's heartbreaks, turmoil, and challenges.

The Preacher tells us that following God is the path to true happiness and fulfillment in our lives. "This is the end of the matter. All has been heard. Fear God and keep his commandments; for this is the whole duty of man" (Eccl. 12:13).

But he also tells young people to rejoice in their lives and strength. "Let your heart cheer you in the days of your youth, and walk in the ways of your heart, and in the sight of your eyes" (Eccl. 11:9). The Preacher probably would tell Allison, Jeremy, and Emma to treasure their dreams and work for their goals. It's what we humans are wired to do: pursue our goals and follow our passions. But he would add, don't fool yourself into thinking that getting into Harvard, playing in the NBA, or becoming a Gamma Phi Beta will alone bring you lasting joy. Believing that everything will be great if you can just achieve your vision of personal success is like trying to reach the end of the rainbow: you'll never get there.

Life will always have frustrations, struggles, and heartbreaks. If we turn inward and bring God into our hearts and lives, we can dwell in that place of joy, peace, and contentment that we all seek.

The Preacher closes his book with a final word of advice: reach out to God before you grow old, before "the light, the moon, and the stars are darkened, and the clouds return after the rain" and before "the dust returns to the earth as it was, and the spirit returns to God who gave it" (Eccl. 12:2, 7). In other words, don't wait until your life is almost over, wasting your time here on earth chasing after the wind, before you surrender yourself to God. Embrace the Lord in your youth, while you still have your life ahead of you and can enjoy the wonderful blessings that come from turning your heart over to our Heavenly Father.

WHAT DO YOU THINK?

- Do you ever catch yourself thinking: "If only I could __, my life would be so happy"? What sorts of things fill in the blank for you?
- Where do you draw the line between having worthy life goals versus putting your hope in things of the world that will never bring true or lasting joy?
- Ecclesiastes seems to say: "I have spent my life chasing rainbows, so I want to help you avoid wasting your life doing the same. Keep God in your hearts from an early age, and your life will be full of joy and meaning." Do you think it's easy to take that advice and learn from the Preacher's experiences? Or does everyone need to learn through trial and error? Is there a middle ground?

Chapter 29

GOD: THE ULTIMATE FIRE RETARDANT

(DANIEL 1–3)

Around 600 BC, Nebuchadnezzar ruled over the kingdom of Babylon. As many power-hungry rulers do, Nebuchadnezzar set out to conquer and control as much of the world as his armies could reach, and that included the kingdom of Judah. His armies eventually destroyed Jerusalem, including the temple built by Solomon, and forced the Jewish people to live under Babylonian rule.

To help cement their control, the Babylonians would remove many of the people in their conquered territories, scattering them into unfamiliar lands and forcing them to give up their government, customs, traditions, and religion. They started with the smartest and most skilled people, bringing them to Babylon to train them to serve the Babylonian government.

Many young Jewish men were brought to Babylon in this way. One of them, Daniel, became the king's favorite when he correctly interpreted several of King Nebuchadnezzar's dreams. To repay Daniel for this great service, Nebuchadnezzar appointed him and three of his buddies, Shadrach, Meshach, and Abednego, to leadership positions within the Babylonian empire.

Nebuchadnezzar then embarked on a major public works project. He built a huge golden idol and then called all his governors, judges, and other officials to witness the great unveiling. At this grand event, Nebuchadnezzar's spokesman announced that the king had ordered that whenever anyone anywhere heard the sound of music, they had to fall down and worship the idol. That was a bit weird, but here's the really scary part: anyone who didn't fall down and worship the idol would be thrown into the king's fiery furnace.

Most people didn't want to end up like a burnt piece of toast, so they dutifully complied. Except for Shadrach, Meshach, and Abednego. Unfortunately for them, one of the local snitches ratted them out to the king. Nebuchadnezzar demanded that the three be brought to him immediately.

The king asked Shadrach, Meshach, and Abednego if there had been some kind of misunderstanding and gave them a chance to change their minds. But the three men replied something to the effect of: "No, King. It wasn't an accident that we refused to worship that gaudy piece of junk you plopped out there in the middle of nowhere. It was quite deliberate. We will only worship one God, the true God of Israel."

This made Nebuchadnezzar hotter than his own furnace. He ordered his henchmen to turn up the temperature in the furnace and make it seven times hotter than normal. He wanted to send a clear message: NOBODY disses Nebuchadnezzar.

The fiery furnace was prepared and the king's mightiest soldiers tied up the three men and threw them in. The roaring inferno was so hot that the soldiers were incinerated just getting close enough to toss in Shadrach, Meshach, and Abednego.

The king was hanging around watching, clearly wanting to see some real suffering, but he nearly fell off his throne when he saw three men walking around in the middle of the fiery blaze. Even more shocking, Nebuchadnezzar could see a fourth guy walking around with them.

"Help me out here," the king said to his minions. "Didn't we just tie up three guys and throw them in the fire?"

"Yep, that's what we did," they told him.

"Then why do I see *four* men, walking around loose in that fire?" And the "appearance of the fourth is like a son of the gods" (Dan. 3:25).

Nebuchadnezzar's curiosity got the better of him, so he moved as close as he dared to the edge of the furnace and hollered, "Shadrach, Meshach, and Abednego, you servants of the Most High God, come out, and come here" (Dan. 3:26).

The three stepped out of the furnace without a mark on them; not even their eyebrows were singed. The fire had not damaged their clothes at all; in fact, they didn't even smell like smoke! While the Bible doesn't tell us what Shadrach, Meshach, and Abednego said when they stepped out of the fire, we can only hope they gave Nebuchadnezzar a little poke, something like: "Hey, King, it was a bit drafty in there. I think I caught a chill. Do you have a sweater I can borrow?"

But we do know what Nebuchadnezzar said. The same king who had been so enraged just a bit earlier because these three men had dared to cross him, said, "Blessed be the God of Shadrach, Meshach, and Abednego, who has sent his angel and delivered his servants who trusted in him" (Dan. 3:28). You have to give Nebuchadnezzar credit for admitting when he was wrong.

The king then promised that no one would ever ask Shadrach, Meshach, and Abednego to worship anyone or anything except their God. In fact, Nebuchadnezzar gave the three promotions and proclaimed that from then on, anyone who spoke badly of the God of Shadrach, Meshach, and Abednego would be "cut in pieces, and their houses shall be made a dunghill" (Dan. 3:29). The "dunghill" piece was clearly just for effect, since nobody would care if their house got transformed into a pile of poop after they had just been chopped up like a Vidalia onion.

Shadrach, Meshach, and Abednego knew they were risking their lives when they refused to worship Nebuchadnezzar's idol, but they did it anyway. Through the centuries, thousands of followers of the one true God have taken similar risks, and not all have been rescued like Shadrach, Meshach, and Abednego were. We call the Christians who were killed for their faith "martyrs," and we often wonder why they risked everything for their beliefs.

Well, for these brave souls, God wasn't just a distant concept or a comforting fairy tale that you pull off the shelf when you're feeling down or worried about the afterlife. For them, God was real, immediate, and existed at the center of their very souls. Renouncing their faith just wasn't an option.

Saint Stephen is considered to be the first martyr of the Christian church. After Jesus' resurrection, Stephen openly criticized the Jewish leaders for rejecting Jesus as the Messiah. As he was speaking to them, Stephen "looked up ... into heaven, and saw the glory of God, and Jesus standing on the right hand of God" (Acts 7:55). When he described the scene to the Jewish leaders, they became so enraged that they stoned him to death. Stephen's clear vision of God the Father and Jesus in all their glory in heaven demonstrates the undeniable and immediate presence of God in his life. His final words, just before he died, also were a testament to his undying devotion to God: "Lord, don't hold this sin against them!" (Acts 7:60).

Saint Stephen and other Christian martyrs were blessed with the courage to lay down their lives in order to bring glory to the Lord. Their brave actions ensured their walk with God in the radiance of his magnificent light, as did Shadrach, Meshach, and Abednego.

In our lives, we will all face a time when we have to decide whether we'll stand by God or turn our backs on him. We probably won't be risking our lives for our faith, but there will be some price to pay, such as being embarrassed or rejected when we stand up for what we believe in. When we're in that moment of decision, we can always rationalize disavowing God by telling ourselves that we need to "go along to get along. And, besides, what difference does it really make anyway?"

We're all pretty good at justifying ourselves when we want to take the easy way out. But deep down inside, we know that giving in to pressure to turn our back on God will damage our spiritual well-being. As we're reminded in the book of Matthew, we should worry less about the people who can kill our body and be more afraid of the people who could kill our souls (Matt. 10:28).

So, how far would you go to stand by our Lord?

WHAT DO YOU THINK?

- How far *would* you go to stand up for God? Would you put your life on the line?
- In today's world, how are we pressured to turn our backs on God and worship "idols"?
- Have you ever professed your faith when you knew it would have negative consequences for you? Would you do it again?

Chapter 30

NICE KITTY, KITTY ...

(DANIEL 6)

After King Nebuchadnezzar died, the kingdom of Babylon was conquered by the Medes and the Persians. The new king, Darius, quickly appointed three presidents to supervise 120 governors who would oversee various parts of the kingdom. Because Daniel had a reputation for being a highly effective and trustworthy leader, King Darius chose him to be one of the three presidents.

It didn't take long for Daniel to prove himself to be the best leader in the kingdom, so Darius started thinking about putting him in charge of all of the other leaders. The other presidents and governors weren't too happy about that, so they began trying to figure out a way to get rid of Daniel.

But Daniel was so honest and hard-working that it was hard for the bad guys to come up with any reason to turn the king against him. That is, until they noticed that Daniel prayed to his God three times every day. This gave them an idea for an evil plan to take Daniel down. First, they went to Darius and buttered him up: "Oh, King, you are so great and mighty. In fact, we think you should do something to help everyone see just how amazing you are." Then they proposed to the king: "Issue an order that no one can worship any god or any human except you for thirty days. And if anyone gets caught worshiping anyone or any god except you, they will be thrown into the lions' den."

Well, the king was so flattered, he barely gave it a second thought. He just signed that decree, which could not be repealed under the legal systems of the Medes and Persians.

As soon as the law was issued, the jealous officials staked out Daniel's place. Now Daniel knew about the new law, but he didn't change his routine. Three times a day, he went into his upstairs room, where the windows opened toward Jerusalem, "got down on his knees and prayed, giving thanks to his God, just as he had done before" (Dan. 6:10).

So the double-crossing officials ran back to Darius and said, "King, we found someone who is breaking your order. He's praying to his God three times a day! He has to be thrown into the lions' den, right?" The king responded, "Well, that is the law."

Then the men told Darius that it was Daniel who had been caught breaking the law, and the king realized he had been tricked. He was greatly distressed and tried to come up with some way around his own law but couldn't figure any way out. And those sneaky officials were not letting up the pressure.

So Darius reluctantly ordered that Daniel be thrown into the lions' den. But first the king offered him some hopeful words: "Your God whom you serve continually, he will deliver you." (Dan. 6:16). That night, Darius felt so bad about Daniel he could hardly sleep. Early the next morning, he jumped out of bed, ran over to the lions' den, and called out to Daniel, hoping that he had miraculously survived the night. Relief flooded the king when he got a reply.

"O king, live forever," Daniel called. "My God has sent his angel, and has shut the lions' mouths, and they have not hurt me, because innocence was found in me before him; and also before you, O king, I have done no harm" (Dan. 6:21–22). The king was overjoyed, especially when they removed Daniel from the lions' den and discovered he wasn't injured at all, not even a scratch.

Then King Darius ordered Daniel's conniving accusers to be thrown into the lions' den, along with their wives and children, and all died a quick but brutal death. Darius then proclaimed that Daniel's God was holy and powerful and decreed that everyone in his whole kingdom should respect the God of Israel.

The story of Daniel and the lions' den is another Old Testament account of God protecting one of his devoted followers. It also highlights an unfortunate fact about our world: people who don't have God in their lives often target people of faith whose only crime is remaining true to the Lord. In all respects, Daniel was an honorable and hard-working guy who was beyond reproach, whom God had blessed with success, prosperity, and the king's favor. The nonbelievers who surrounded Daniel were jealous of those blessings, and they let their jealousy overtake them. And they attempted to use Daniel's undying devotion to God as the catalyst for having him snuffed out, once and for all.

But, just like in this story, ultimately, God will bring justice to both the faithful and the wicked. As it says in the book of Proverbs: "Most certainly, the evil man will not be unpunished but the offspring of the righteous will be delivered" (Prov. 11:21).

WHAT DO YOU THINK?

- The king's presidents and governors were incredibly jealous of Daniel. The fact is, most of us struggle with jealousy at one time or another. Where do these feelings come from?
- We can always pray that God will help us get over feelings of jealousy or envy. What are some other steps we might take to overcome those feelings?
- Was the king entirely innocent of any wrongdoing? What could he have done differently? Why do you think he went along with the proposed law?

Chapter 31

JONAH: MAN OF GOD, OR ACID REFLUX?

(JONAH 1–4)

Every now and then, we all need to find a nice, quiet place where we can reflect on what we've been doing with our lives, where our lives are taking us, and what God wants from us. And if we don't take the initiative to find that space on our own, sometimes the Good Lord will find it for us. Just like he did for the prophet Jonah. Unfortunately for Jonah, that nice, quiet place was somewhere between the esophagus and large intestine of a hungry fish.

Our story begins when God commanded Jonah to travel to Nineveh, a big city that had fallen into widespread sin and corruption. God wanted Jonah to tell the Ninevites that he was furious with their wicked behavior and was planning to turn their urban cesspool into the next Sodom and Gomorrah unless they shaped up *and fast*. However, traveling to Nineveh to bear bad news to these degenerates wasn't high on Jonah's bucket list, so he bought a one-way ticket for a boat ride to Tarshish, which was in the complete opposite direction of

Nineveh. You have to wonder, did Jonah seriously think God wouldn't notice?

On the way to Tarshish, Jonah's boat sailed into a fierce storm. To keep the boat afloat, the crew threw cargo overboard, but the seas kept raging, and the future looked bleak. The storm was so bad that the sailors began to suspect someone on board must have done something to really annoy God. After a thorough investigation, Jonah admitted he had angered God by refusing his assignment and sailing away to Tarshish.

Jonah said to them, "Take me up, and throw me into the sea. Then the sea will be calm for you; for I know that because of me this great storm is on you" (Jonah 1:12). The sailors didn't feel right about pitching Jonah overboard, so they tried their hardest to row to shore. But when the storm grew even fiercer, they abandoned their hero routine and tossed Jonah overboard like a bucket of smelly chum. They did, however, beg God to forgive them for what they were doing. Soon, the seas calmed and the mariners were safe, although still pretty freaked out by the whole experience.

But God had sent a giant fish just for this moment, and it gobbled up Jonah, giving him a distraction-free haven. Sitting inside the creature's belly, Jonah prayed for forgiveness for having defied God and also thanked the Lord for saving him from the raging seas. After three days and three nights, God "spoke to the fish, and it vomited out Jonah on the dry land" (Jonah 2:10).

Then God spoke to Jonah again. "Arise, go to Nineveh, that great city, and preach to it the message that I give you" (Jonah 3:2). And this time, Jonah did just that. He traveled to Nineveh and put the fear of God in its people—literally. Jonah told the people of Nineveh that God was planning to overthrow them in forty days for their wickedness. The people believed Jonah and repented. Even the king got scared and cried out to God for mercy, telling his people to stop their evil and violence. And God saw their reactions, and he offered his mercy, sparing the city of the destruction he had planned.

Jonah clearly was a gifted preacher, convincing a huge wicked city to repent. But his success didn't make him happy at all. Truth be told, Jonah wasn't particularly fond of the Ninevites. In fact, he hated them.

The people of Nineveh were Assyrians, rivals of the Jewish people who had treated them brutally in the past. Jonah would have been happier if the Ninevites had ignored his warning and continued their wicked ways because he wanted to watch God eradicate them from the face of the earth. Seeing that Jonah needed a bit of attitude adjustment, God decided to teach him another lesson.

Jonah had left Nineveh after he finished preaching and was now sitting outside the city so he would have a front-row seat if God changed his mind and decided to destroy Nineveh after all. Jonah built himself a little hut, and the Lord offered up some comfort for Jonah, providing a lush green vine that grew up over the hut, completely protecting him from the blazing sun.

Jonah was extremely grateful for the vine. But the next day God sent a worm to eat away at the vine, leaving Jonah to sizzle in the hot sun like a french fry. He got so overheated, he fainted. When Jonah regained consciousness, he was so angry that he prayed to God to just let him die.

Of course, God was at the ready for this teaching moment. He told Jonah something like: "You have a lot of nerve carrying on like the ultimate drama queen over the death of a silly plant. Especially when you wanted me to kill 120,000 Ninevites—actual human beings that were created by none other than yours truly—just because you have a bone to pick with them. You need to put in perspective, my friend, how you value human life. Or else you might find yourself in the belly of another fish. And, next time, you won't be so lucky to get puked out of its mouth. On the next go-round, you might just find yourself shooting out the other end as oceanic fertilizer."

Presumably, Jonah got the point.

This story teaches us two important lessons. First, when God calls, you need to answer. That call could be to do something as simple as sharing your faith with a friend or volunteering for a church project or helping someone in need. Or the call could be to do something more demanding, like missionary work or entering the seminary. God does have a specific plan for each of us, and we will only experience true joy and meaning in our lives if we answer God's call. Of course, we have the right to decline. We also have the option to close the door on God altogether and pretend that he doesn't even exist. But you must realize that God holds us accountable for our actions—and also for our inaction. When we try to hide from the Lord and refuse his calling for our lives, we probably won't be swallowed up by a giant fish. But there will be consequences. At the very least, we'll feel the emptiness that comes from living a life separate from God.

The book of Jonah also provides a second lesson, although lots of people miss this one: God does not respond well when we wish harm or misfortune on other people—even our enemies. Jesus taught us that you must "love your enemies, bless those who curse you, do good to those who hate you, and pray for those who mistreat you and persecute you, that you may be children of your Father who is in heaven" (Matt. 5:44–45). As with the Ninevites, God loves every person that he created and, although he punishes those who do evil, he gives everyone an opportunity to repent and come home to him.

At one time or another, most of us fall into that dark place where we let our anger and resentment toward someone get the best of us. But when we conclude that other people are worthy of God's punishment, we need to remind ourselves that we have only a tiny glimpse of their life and motives. Only God fully knows what is inside the hearts and minds of people who have hurt us. So, it's not for us to judge who should receive God's blessings and who deserves punishment. Our job is to remain obedient to the Lord and to love everyone, as he has commanded. If our enemies repent and receive God's blessing, we should rejoice and be glad.

WHAT DO YOU THINK?

- Have you ever tried to run away and hide from God like Jonah did? What prompted you to do that? Were you refusing to do what God wanted you to do? Or were you just angry with him?
- Jonah came back to God after he was swallowed by a giant fish. How has God brought you back to him? What other methods does he use to bring us back?
- Have you ever had a hard time letting go of anger or resentment of someone or a group of people? Did you wish that something bad would happen to that person? How can you overcome those feelings?

PART TWO:
THE NEW TESTAMENT

Jesus said: "Come to me, all you who labor and are heavily burdened, and I will give you rest. Take my yoke upon you and learn from me, for I am gentle and humble in heart; and you will find rest for your souls. For my yoke is easy, and my burden is light."

(MATTHEW 11:28–30)

Chapter 32

COUSINS, AND THEIR TWO VERY SPECIAL BABIES

(LUKE 1:5–66)

In the days of the Roman Empire, in the land of Judea, there lived a priest named Zacharias. He and his wife, Elizabeth, were devoted to the Lord and led mostly happy lives, although they both were sad that they had never been blessed with a child. One day, Zacharias was praying in the Jewish temple when he was startled to see a man standing near him in what had been an empty room. Turns out that it wasn't a man, it was the angel Gabriel, who had been sent by God to deliver a message.

Gabriel told Zacharias that he and Elizabeth would soon have a son, and they should name him John. The angel told Zacharias that his son would be "great in the sight of the Lord … and filled with the Holy Spirit, even from his mother's womb. He will turn many of the children of Israel to the Lord their God" (Luke 1:15–16).

Zacharias just couldn't quite believe this great news. You see, he and Elizabeth were way too old to have children, at least without some serious divine intervention. So he responded to Gabriel with something to the effect of, "Are you crazy? My wife and I are older than King Tut's grandmother. How could we possibly have kids? That ship sailed a LONG time ago!"

Of course, Gabriel gave Zacharias the "everything's possible with God" speech. But, because Zacharias doubted him, Gabriel told him he would lose the ability to speak until the baby was born. As Gabriel foretold, Zacharias became mute, and Elizabeth became pregnant.

About six months later, Gabriel paid another surprise visit. This time, he did his appearing-from-nowhere act for a young woman named Mary. Gabriel told Mary she would become pregnant and "give birth to a son, and shall name him 'Jesus.' He will be great and will be called the Son of the Most High" (Luke 1:31–32).

Mary was pretty skeptical because she couldn't understand how she could possibly become pregnant. Although she was engaged to a man named Joseph, they were waiting to get married before being intimate. In other words, she was a virgin.

But Gabriel told her not to worry. "The Holy Spirit will come on you, and the power of the Most High will overshadow you. Therefore also the holy one who is born from you will be called the Son of God" (Luke 1:35). Then Gabriel tried to reassure Mary by telling her about Elizabeth, Mary's cousin, who was too old to have a baby but was now six months pregnant. "Nothing spoken by God is impossible," Gabriel said.

"I am God's servant," Mary said, letting the angel know that she was ready for anything. But she also needed to talk to somebody who might understand. So Mary packed her bags and traveled to the hill country of Judah to spend some time with Elizabeth, her older, wiser cousin. When Mary arrived and called out a greeting, Elizabeth's baby leaped inside her womb and Elizabeth was filled with the Holy Spirit. She proclaimed to Mary: "Blessed are you among women, and blessed is the fruit of your womb! Why am I so favored, that the mother of my Lord should come to me?" (John 1:42–43).

Mary stayed with Elizabeth for the next three months, no doubt helping Elizabeth with some of the household chores during the final stage of Elizabeth's pregnancy. And Mary must have been soaking up her older cousin's spiritual and emotional support during what had to be a magnificent but scary time. We can only imagine how the two must have talked during those three months, especially since Zacharias wasn't saying anything. One of their conversations probably sounded something like this.

Mary: Pssst! Hey cuz, wake up.

Elizabeth: Mary? What is it? Is something wrong?

Mary: No, no, I'm fine. I just can't sleep. I'm just feeling really anxious—about my life, my baby.

Elizabeth: Oh, sweetie, that's totally understandable. Just remember, all you can do is try your best. And then trust that the Lord will take care of everything else. It's going to be fine.

Mary: I know. And don't think I'm complaining—I'm really not. It's just that I'm worried that I won't be a good mother. It wasn't that long ago that I was a kid myself—sometimes

I feel like I'm still a kid. And just being a regular mother would be hard enough. But having God's child? I don't even understand what that means.

Elizabeth: It means you were chosen by our Lord and Creator, among every other woman who ever lived or ever will live, to bear God's son. And raise him to be the man who will bring salvation to God's people.

Mary: Gee, when you put it that way—no pressure, huh?

Elizabeth: I know, right? Just remember, while we can't know the mind of God, the Lord knows every single thing about us, inside and out. So he knew exactly what he was doing when he picked you.

Mary: You always make so much sense. Don't get me wrong, I really meant it when I said that my "soul magnifies the Lord" and that my "spirit has rejoiced in God my Savior" (Luke 1:46–47). I love God so much, I want my whole life to bring glory to him. It's just that, when I pictured my future life with Joseph, I envisioned my kids playing in the yard and helping with chores. I thought about making nice dinners together, tucking them into their beds at night—you know, a quiet, happy, *normal* life.

Elizabeth: Well, you could still have that.

Mary: I'm not so sure. I know in my heart that my child will have a very hard life. It will be a glorious and magnificent life, but he'll suffer greatly. And the thought of that breaks my heart.

Elizabeth: To be honest, I've been feeling the same way about my baby. But the Lord has a plan for all of us, including our children. And I have faith that whatever comes our way—or their way—will be for the best. It will be part of God's plan. And there will be a happy ending, so long as we put our faith in the Lord.

Mary: I guess I just needed to hear you say that. I pray that I won't let him down.

Elizabeth: Now listen to me, cousin. You are going to be just wonderful. And someday our boys will cross paths and it will be a grand and glorious day.

Mary: I hope you're right.

Elizabeth: You know, our time here on earth is short. And there is no better way to spend it than in the Lord's service. But, when life gets hard, remember, God will always be there for you. And so will I.

After spending much quality time with Elizabeth, Mary went home. And not long after that, Elizabeth gave birth to her son. When friends asked the baby's name, Zacharias spelled it out on a tablet: "His name is John" (Luke 1:63). Immediately Zacharias could speak again, and he started pouring out nine months of praises to God. And all was good.

WHAT DO YOU THINK?

- Why do you think God chose a virgin as the mother of his son?
- Do you think it was just a coincidence that the mothers of Jesus and John the Baptist were relatives? Was that part of God's plan? If so, why?
- Many biblical scholars believe Mary was in her early teens when she became pregnant with Jesus, as that was the customary age of marriage at the time. What sorts of feelings do you think Mary experienced in the months before Jesus' birth?

Chapter 33

DO ME A SOLID
AND SPRINKLE SOME
OF THAT FRANKINCENSE
OVER BY THE PIG STALLS

(MATTHEW 1:18–25; 2:1–15; LUKE 1:26–38; 2:1–20)

If you're ever feeling sorry for yourself because you weren't born into a rich family with a big fancy house, luxurious cars, or lots of expensive toys, consider poor Jesus. You could hardly imagine anyone starting out in more humble surroundings. Mary and Joseph had to travel to Bethlehem because the Roman emperor ordered everyone to return to their hometowns so they could be counted in the latest census. The couple made the trip by donkey, which is anything but comfortable especially if, like Mary, you're nine months pregnant.

After days on the road, no doubt dying to collapse in a nice comfy bed, Mary and Joseph arrived in Bethlehem. Imagine their disappointment when they couldn't find a single inn that wasn't completely booked up. This was especially alarming because Mary was telling Joseph that the baby was coming—and soon! With no other option, they settled in a stable where animals were kept.

Of course, there was no bassinet lying around the old barn. So, when Jesus was born, Mary and Joseph placed him in a manger. In other words, the kid's first bed was a trough where the farm animals would slobber over whatever gruel was on the menu. Although the baby's first digs were lowbrow, his birth announcement was pretty awesome. The angels lit up the sky and sang to a bunch of shepherds out in the field. The shepherds then rushed over to the stable to see baby Jesus. Thankfully, three wise men from the East brought a little majesty to the event. But let's be honest, Jesus probably didn't have much use for the gifts they brought: gold, frankincense, and myrrh. No doubt, he would have preferred a nice teddy bear or baby blanket.

So why would God have arranged for his one and only son, and our savior, to start his life in such deplorable conditions? It was to make plain who Jesus was—and who he was not. The Jewish people believed their Messiah, or savior, would come as a powerful king to liberate them from Roman oppression and bring peace and prosperity here on earth. But God had bigger plans than just another earthly king who would champion the political cause of the Jewish people. God was sending Jesus into this world to save the souls of all God's children for all eternity.

Jesus shows us that the road to salvation and ultimately to heaven is not built on political or military power, earthly riches, personal success, or social status. Instead, salvation comes when we surrender our hearts to God and commit ourselves to a life filled with kindness, humility, and love for one another. The hardships Jesus faced, right from the time of his birth, remind us that we cannot claim that our lives are just too difficult or filled with too many challenges for us to follow the ways of God.

The Bible teaches us that Jesus endured just about every torment one could suffer, including poverty, rejection, physical pain, betrayal, torture, and ultimately death. And yet Jesus lived his entire life without sinning. So, when the Lord calls us to fulfill his plan for our own lives, we are reminded by the birth, life, and death of Jesus to put aside the excuses and answer God's call.

WHAT DO YOU THINK?

- How do our images of our Christmas nativity scenes differ from what Mary and Joseph actually experienced?
- Do you sometimes blame your family or your circumstances for choices you make in life? Do you think your ability to achieve certain goals is hampered because of where you were born or how much money your family makes?
- In addition to Jesus, can you name some people who overcame humble beginnings or major challenges to achieve greatness in this world?

Chapter 34

LOOK AT THE BRIGHT SIDE: AT LEAST HE DIDN'T JOIN THE CIRCUS

(LUKE 2:39–52)

The book of Luke tells how twelve-year-old Jesus slipped away from his family to hang out at the temple in Jerusalem while his parents were on the road to Nazareth. Other than his birth, this is the only glimpse the Bible gives us of the first thirty years of Jesus' life. So it must have special significance in helping us to understand who Jesus truly was.

Imagine how this situation might have played out if ancient Rome had child protective services akin to those of a current-day Department of Social Services (DSS). The proceedings are about to begin; let's watch.

Judge Magistrate: Hear ye, hear ye! By the authority vested in me by our Imperator Augustus Caesar, I call this hearing of the Department of Social Services to order. The purpose of this proceeding is to decide whether the court should remove the minor, Jesus, from the custody of his parents,

Joseph and Mary of Nazareth. The DSS investigator asserts that Joseph and Mary are unfit parents by virtue of their alleged child neglect and therefore the minor Jesus should be placed into foster care. I will now read into the record the relevant facts as stated in the report and then allow the child's mother to be heard. Are we all clear on that?

Joseph: Yes, Your Honor.

Mary: Yes, sir.

Judge Magistrate: The petition for removal of custody states that the minor is twelve years old. He had accompanied his parents, Joseph and Mary, on their annual pilgrimage from their home in Nazareth to Jerusalem to celebrate the Jewish holiday of Passover. When the holiday was over, Joseph and Mary commenced their travel back home with family and friends who also lived in Nazareth. It wasn't until they had traveled an entire day that the allegedly neglectful parents, Joseph and Mary, realized that the minor Jesus was not with them. Upon learning of the child's absence, they immediately returned to Jerusalem. They searched for three days before they found Jesus in the Jewish temple conversing with religious leaders. The petition charges that no fit parent would leave their child in a large city and embark on their travels home. The DSS Investigator requests that this administrative court deny any further custody of the child by Joseph and Mary until they have undergone extensive parenting training and can satisfy this court that, in the future, they will exercise sound judgment in the care of the child. At this point in the proceeding, I would like to call the child's mother to respond to these charges. Madam, please take the witness stand and state your name.

Mary: Yes, Your Honor. My name is Mary of Nazareth.

Judge Magistrate: Are you indeed the child's mother?

Mary: Yes, sir.

Judge Magistrate: And is this man, Joseph of Nazareth, the child's father?

Mary: As I am under oath, I must tell the truth. Joseph is not the child's biological father but is Jesus' father by virtue of his marriage to me.

Judge Magistrate: Who is the boy's biological father?

Mary: That would be God, sir.

Judge Magistrate: Did you say God?

Mary: Yes, Your Honor.

Judge Magistrate: You're telling this court that someone like Jupiter or Neptune is the child's natural father?

Mary: No, not a Roman God, but the one and only true god, the God of our forefathers Abraham, Isaac, and Jacob.

Judge Magistrate: Madam, you do realize that one possible ground for losing custody of your child is if you are determined by this court to be a certifiable wing nut? But let's leave that aside for now. All right, did you, or did you not, leave Jesus, your firstborn child, in Jerusalem while you traveled back home, completely unaware that he was not with you or your husband, Joseph?

Mary: Yes, Your Honor. I'm afraid that is true.

Judge Magistrate: Well, you have been accused of child neglect, which is a pretty serious charge. Do you have anything to say in your own defense?

Mary: I do, Your Honor. First, let me try to explain. Please understand that we are a very modest, humble, and religious family. As such, we live by the traditions of our faith. We are not modern-day people who allow men and women to mix and socialize freely with one another. So, when we travel long distances with many in our group, the women tend to stay together separately from the men, as we did in this case. I assumed Jesus was traveling with Joseph and the other men since he is approaching the age of manhood. Joseph believed Jesus would travel with me and the other mothers and the young children. You see, Jesus is between the age of boyhood and manhood, so he could have been with either group, and Joseph and I each assumed that our son was with the other. However, the moment we learned that Jesus wasn't with us, we rushed back to Jerusalem and searched high and low until we found him.

Judge Magistrate: Well, that might explain why you didn't realize right away that he wasn't with you. But it's odd that the boy cared so little for you that he chose to stay in the temple so many days without even looking for you. According to the DSS investigator, this is the behavior of a child who has profound disregard and even resentment toward his parents. I'd like to know what you and your husband did to this child to make him seek refuge in the temple and display such utter contempt for you and his stepfather.

Mary: Your Honor, please understand, Jesus has never been like the other boys. From the time that he was little, he devoted most of his free time to spiritual matters. I do not believe he remained in the temple for all of those days to hide from Joseph and me. In fact, he told us he assumed we would know where to find him. When we finally located him, his exact words were: "Why were you looking for me? Didn't you know that I must be in my Father's house?" (Luke 2:49). Of course, Joseph and I were furious with him at first, but we also had to feel some pride when the Jewish leaders told us about his impressive religious knowledge and insights. He asked them many tough questions, I guess. As crazy as this sounds, I feel Jesus was honoring us by staying behind in the temple.

Judge Magistrate: Honoring you? How so?

Mary: By completely devoting himself to his Father in Heaven, his religious studies, and the building of his character through the practice of our Jewish faith. These are the things that Joseph and I have instilled in him since the day he was born.

Judge Magistrate: I see. Do you have anything else to add?

Mary: Well, just that my husband and I love Jesus more than words can describe. But we will humbly accept the judgment of this court, whatever that might be.

Judge Magistrate: Okay, thank you, Madam. At this point, I think it would be helpful for me to hear from the child. Young man, please take the witness stand and then state your name for the record.

Jesus: My name is Jesus of Nazareth.

Judge Magistrate: Let me start by saying your behavior is not at issue here. But I do need to understand why you did what you did because it might have a bearing on whether your parents are fit to have ongoing custody of you. The whole point of this proceeding is to determine what is in your best interests. Do you understand that?

Jesus: Yes, sir.

Judge Magistrate: Good. Then let me start by asking the burning question I have been wondering about. Why would you possibly stay in the temple for an entire five days without giving any thought to your parents? That's the part I don't understand. Did they do something to you along the way that made you resent them? Or at least disregard them?

Jesus: No, sir. I love my mom and dad very much and would never do anything to intentionally hurt them. I couldn't ask for two better parents. And I think it's important to state that I have never considered Joseph as my stepfather. He is my earthly father and I care about him deeply.

Judge Magistrate: So why didn't you leave Jerusalem with your parents? Why did you stay in the temple when you must have known that would cause them much distress?

Jesus: I actually didn't know they had left. Before we traveled to Jerusalem for Passover, I told my parents how excited I was to spend time with the Jewish teachers in the temple to get some of my questions answered about our Jewish forefathers, our traditions, and our faith. My mother was right—I'm different from a lot of the other kids. I devote my life here on earth to matters of the spirit and to the work of my Father in Heaven.

Judge Magistrate: But you're still young. Don't you want to have fun with the other kids and enjoy yourself before you have all of the burdens of being an adult?

Jesus: My enjoyment comes from fulfilling my father's plan for my life. All year, I look forward to Passover so I can go to the temple and learn from our religious leaders in Jerusalem. And now that I'm twelve, I knew I could spend more time conversing with them and discussing matters of our faith. I thought my parents were just giving me extra time to engage with the temple elders.

Judge Magistrate: Okay, but five days? Didn't it seem odd to you that they wouldn't check on you even once for that entire time?

Jesus: When I look back on it now, yes, I guess so. But to be honest, I felt so at home in the temple and was so happy to be immersing myself in my religious studies that I completely lost track of time.

Judge Magistrate: Okay, is there anything else you would like to say to this court?

Jesus: Just that my mother and father are the most honorable, responsible, and loving people that I know. I am so blessed to have them as my parents.

Judge Magistrate: Well, in light of the testimony provided here today, I am going to deny the DSS investigator's request and allow Joseph and Mary of Nazareth to keep custody of Jesus. And, I must say, Jesus, you are a remarkable young man. I expect that you will make your mark on this world, and I look forward to hearing great things about you someday.

Jesus: Thank you, sir.

Mary: Thank you, Your Honor.

Judge Magistrate: I hereby request that the clerk enter the order of this court and call this hearing to a close.

WHAT DO YOU THINK?

- Imagine Jesus as a twelve-year-old in today's world. Do you think he would have an iPhone and poke at it for hours on end? Do you think he would get perfect grades in school? Would you want to hang out with him?
- Why do you think God sent his son into the world when he did? Do you think something about the state of the world 2,000 years ago made it the right time?

Chapter 35

PROUD FATHER, LOYAL SON, HOLY GHOST

(MATTHEW 3; MARK 1:1–11; LUKE 3:21–22)

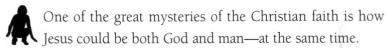 One of the great mysteries of the Christian faith is how Jesus could be both God and man—at the same time.

No question, he was fully human. He ate real food, shed real tears, and bled real blood. He experienced pain, joy, frustration, sadness, and love. And, at least in the physical sense, he died a very human death. However, Jesus also was endowed with some serious God firepower. He was able to heal the sick, walk on water, bring people back from the grave, and even come back to earth following his own death. We also know that Jesus was able to see some things about the future, such as knowing in advance when and how his life would end.

We will never be able to fully comprehend the interplay between Jesus the man and Jesus our God, but the Bible's accounts of his life do shed some light on this mysterious dual nature. One such event was Jesus' baptism, which happened just before he embarked on his public ministry here on earth. In the sacrament of baptism, the "baptizee" comes to the "baptizor," (more properly called the "baptist") as a step toward redemption. The baptist immerses the baptizee in water to symbolize God's washing away of sins.

When Jesus was ready to be baptized, he turned to his cousin, John. You remember John—we met him in chapter 32, right when he was born. This son of Elizabeth and Zacharias grew up to be a mighty man of God, just like the angel Gabriel had predicted. He attracted a lot of attention for his preaching, and many Jewish people headed out to the wilderness of Judea, confessing their sins, and asking John to baptize them in the Jordan River. In fact, John baptized so many people that he has forevermore been known as John the Baptist.

As baptists go, John was pretty rough and tumble. How do we know that? Well, for starters, he ate bugs. Mark 1:6 says, "John was clothed with camel's hair and a leather belt around his waist. He ate locusts and wild honey." And Matthew 3:2 tells us that John stood out in the wilderness, yelling, "Repent, for the Kingdom of Heaven is at hand!" Also, John was not shy about publicly shaming people for their sins, even calling some of the Jewish leaders "offspring of vipers." He told the Jewish people that they had to shape up because the Son of God was about to enter the scene. In this way, John served as a forerunner of Jesus, paving the way for the ministry that would change the world forever.

When Jesus joined the crowds seeking baptism, John initially resisted. "You should be baptizing me," John said, because he recognized Jesus as the Son of God and the Messiah. But Jesus was having none of that. Acknowledging his own humanity, Jesus insisted on being baptized like all other people of faith to "fulfill all righteousness" (Matt. 3:15). So John dutifully complied.

As John was baptizing Jesus, the skies opened up, God's spirit descended from heaven in the form of a dove, and a voice from heaven cried out: "This is my beloved Son, with whom I am well pleased" (Matt. 3:17). The dual nature of Jesus, the man and the divine, was on full display in that moment when a bug-eating, animal-skin-wearing guy dunked Jesus in a river as the heavens opened and the Creator of the universe boomed praise for his much-loved son. No doubt, a glorious sight to behold!

WHAT DO YOU THINK?

- Do you believe baptism is required to get into heaven?
- In your view, what are the most important reasons for baptism?
- When you think about Jesus, do you picture him mostly as the all-knowing and all-powerful God? Or do you see him as human, with the same sorts of thoughts and feelings that all people have?
- When you pray, do you have a mental picture of who you are praying to? Are you praying to God the Father, God the Son (Jesus), or some combination of the two? Does it depend on the circumstances?

Chapter 36

THE DEVIL'S PLAYBOOK: KICK HIM WHEN HE'S DOWN

(MATTHEW 4:1–11; MARK 1:12–13; LUKE 4:1–13)

Right after Jesus was baptized, the Holy Spirit led him back into the wilderness, but this time he was all alone for forty days and forty nights, praying and fasting. And that's when the Prince of Darkness came to call and did his best to tempt Jesus to turn his back on God.

This encounter with Satan gives us further insight into Jesus' dual nature, as both God and man. The Devil swooped in when he knew Jesus would be in a vulnerable physical state. The human part of Jesus would have been hungry and weak and tired. But Jesus' divine nature also became evident in those forty days of prayer and alignment with God, which we can see in the way he responded to Satan. The encounter went something like this.

Satan: Hey bro, I see you've lost some weight. Trying to get in shape for swimsuit season?

Jesus: You're a real comedian, you know that? Don't you have some natural disaster or deadly epidemic that you need to conjure up? Why don't you slither away and crawl back under the rock that you came from.

Satan: Well, I see *someone* has a bad case of the hangries. You might want to consider using your godly powers to turn these desert rocks into loaves of bread. Maybe if you engage in some serious carb-loading, you'll regain what little sense of humor you had before you started this ridiculous hunger strike.

Jesus: "Man shall not live by bread alone, but by every word that proceeds out of God's mouth" (Matt. 4:4).

Satan: Yeah, whatever. How about you and I take a little trip? Let's head up to the top of this tower on the temple in Jerusalem. We're up pretty high—I hope you don't get a nose-bleed. I don't have any tissues on me.

Jesus: So what's your point?

Satan: Okay, let's cut right to the chase. Right now, you are in physical agony, probably in the final stages of complete star-vation. And if you survive this whole ugly ordeal here, things are only going to get worse for you.

Jesus: What are you talking about?

Satan: You know as well as I do that your cold-hearted Father in Heaven has a pretty miserable future planned for you here on earth. And we both know it will end in some horribly pain-ful and humiliating death. So why not put an end to it all right now and jump?

Jesus: And why would I do that?

Satan: Because, if God truly gives a rat's behind about you, he'll catch you and make everything okay. Go ahead, don't be a chicken. Jump!

Jesus: You are unbelievable. How did a guy like you, who had everything going for him, end up so screwed up? Anyway, you're right about one thing. Right now, I'm suffering more than I ever thought possible and can barely stand the pain. But I'm not going to throw in the towel on my life. And I'm also not going to put my Father in Heaven to the test just to see if he'll catch me. One of the reasons he sent me here is to share in the human experience with all of my brothers and sisters here on earth. Every person who ever lived in this world has suffered greatly at one time or another, and so must I.

Satan: Why should you suffer? You're just as much God as the old geezer in heaven. It's not fair that he should get to sit up there on his throne all comfy and happy while he watches you writhe in pain in the blistering heat of this godforsaken wilderness.

Jesus: He's not "happy" watching me suffer. I have no doubt his heart is breaking right now, just as it does every time he has to watch any one of his children suffer.

Satan: Yeah, right. Then why doesn't he do something about it? Why does he just sit there and let you and the rest of humanity suffer? I think he's a sick dude. And you're just a sucker. So prove me wrong and jump!

Jesus: God does sometimes step in and rescue his children when things get really bad. But not always. He lets things play out here on earth, even during the really tough times, so his children will realize this world is not the ultimate source of true or lasting joy. Real happiness and fulfillment only come when you turn your life over to him. And struggling through the challenges here on earth—many of which can be very painful—allows us to grow and become strong.

Satan: Well, what about you? Aren't you without sin? Why are you so willing to accept punishment that's more befitting of those wretched little humans?

Jesus: I was sent here to earth to teach the ways of my Father. Not as an all-powerful deity, but as a living, breathing person, who fully shares in the human experience. If God keeps me from suffering or feeling the pains of human existence, then there wouldn't have been much point in my coming in the first place. I am here as an innocent lamb to be sacrificed for my brothers and sisters. After I die a physical death and rise from the grave to heaven, the world will see that my Father's love and my love for all of his children will forever reign supreme over death, despair, sin, and evil. In other words, over *you*!

Satan: Blah, blah, blah. Well, before you bore *me* to death, I have one more place to take you. ... How do you like the view from this mountain? Look out, you can see all the kingdoms on earth. Take a look, Jesus. Aren't they magnificent? All of these kingdoms can be yours. I will make you ruler of the world. All you have to do is bow down and worship me.

Jesus: I didn't come here to rule this world. I came for a much bigger purpose than that. My Father sent me here to open the doors to heaven and bring salvation to people who surrender their lives to him and live according to his word. No matter how bad my pain becomes or how tempting your offers might be, I'll never turn my back on my Father in Heaven or his plan for my life.

Satan: Sorry, I think I nodded off when you started blathering on about why you came to earth—as if I care. Anywho, as much as this has been a boatload of laughs, I'm late for a wild boar roast where I'm the honored guest. I don't want to keep my fans waiting. I heard they're serving the roast with a delicious apricot demiglace, a side of loaded mashed potatoes, and chocolate cheesecake for dessert. Oh, I'm sorry. Am I making you hungry?

Jesus: Go away.

Satan: Fine, be that way. I'll be back when you least expect me. And, of course, you always know how to find me: just close your eyes, click your heels together three times and say, "There's no place like hell, there's no place like hell, there's no place like hell." I'll appear before you can say Moses' toeses. Then I'll share with you all of the wicked delights of the Dark Side—it'll be magical. But, for now, tootles!

Jesus' time out in the desert didn't end with the heavens opening up or God the Father making a grand proclamation like he did after the baptism. This temptation saga was a fairly private affair that required Jesus to check his godly powers at the door and suffer the agony of being fully human. But when Satan showed up, Jesus' holy and sanctified nature shined like a beacon, fortifying him to reject the temptations of this world and stand unwavering in his devotion to his Heavenly Father. And Matthew 4:11 tells us that, when the Devil left Jesus alone, the "angels came and served him," probably taking care of Jesus' human needs while reaffirming his divine status.

WHAT DO YOU THINK?

- If Satan tempted you in the same way he tempted Jesus, which of the three temptations would be most difficult for you to resist? Why?
- In what ways have you faced temptations similar to Jesus' first test: food for a starving man?
- How about the second temptation, testing God to see if he'll confirm his love for you?
- What about the third? How does the lure of power and wealth tempt you today?
- When you are tempted to sin, do you visualize a mental image of the Devil taunting you?
- What techniques work best for you to help you resist temptation?

Chapter 37

A ROBIN PUSHES HER BABY CHICK OUT OF THE NEST

(JOHN 2:1–11)

Once in a while, God does something that leaves us scratching our heads, wondering what the heck he was thinking. Take, for example, the very first public miracle Jesus performed, the one that would jump-start his career as the Messiah.

It all started when Jesus and his mother and his newly called disciples were invited to a wedding in the town of Cana. In Jesus' time, weddings didn't last for just an afternoon or an evening. They were huge bashes that often continued for days, sometimes an entire week. So the bride and groom needed to make sure they had plenty of food and drinks on hand. Well, at this particular wedding, either the hosts were terrible party planners or their guests were especially "thirsty," because the unthinkable happened: they ran out of wine.

Back in those days, wine was an important ingredient for any halfway decent celebration. So this wedding feast was about to die a premature death unless someone could come up with a boatload of wine, and quick. Running short of wine meant the bride and groom and their families would suffer the ultimate humiliation of being bad hosts, not to mention cheapskates.

Jesus' mother caught wind of the wine situation and wasted no time in bringing it to her son's attention. At first, Jesus sounded a bit annoyed, like she had just asked him to take out the garbage in the middle of his favorite TV show. His actual words were: "Woman, what does that have to do with you and me? My hour has not yet come" (John 2:4). But Mary just smiled and told the servants to do whatever Jesus told them to do.

So Jesus did the right thing that would make his mother happy. He told the servants to fill six 25-gallon stone pots with water, then told them to draw out some liquid. And then, sure enough, he turned the water into wine. But it was not just any wine, it was *really good* wine. The local wine expert said it was so delicious that he couldn't believe the hosts had saved it for last. So the guests had plenty of wine, the party was a smashing success, and the bride and groom hopefully lived happily ever after.

So that was the first miracle? Transforming water into wine so a bunch of guests celebrating a wedding could keep on partying? Really, God? Whatever happened to healing the sick, calming the seas, or bringing people back from the dead?

Also, why did Jesus tell Mary that his hour had "not yet come"? Is one time better than another to turn water into wine? (For that matter, is there a bad time for making wine?) Well, his timing comment probably had nothing to do with wine at all. Jesus likely knew his first public miracle would get immediate attention. The word about him would start to spread, and his ministry would be under way. And, although it would ultimately end in glory through his resurrection, that would come only after Jesus suffered ridicule, humiliation, physical pain, and death.

Jesus' resistance to his mother probably just shows his human side, the man hoping he could delay this step just a little bit longer. But Mary knew God had a very vital plan for her son, though she probably didn't have a clear picture of how it would wind up. So she set the wheels in motion for Jesus to fulfill his purpose on earth.

Although we cannot read the mind of God, Jesus' first miracle shows us that God cares even about the small stuff in our lives. Although the bride and groom would have survived even if the wine had run out, it mattered a great deal to them, which is why Mary brought the problem to Jesus. The embarrassment they would have suffered was real, and Jesus felt compassion for them and intervened with a miracle.

As Christians, we should pray often and for everything, no matter how small or inconsequential it might seem (see Phil. 4:6; Luke 12:6–7). Whether it's having enough food for your party, struggling with your schoolwork, being cut from the basketball team, or feeling unfairly treated in your friendships—no matter how small you may think your problem is, God wants you to bring it to him. Even challenges that are not life-threatening or long-lasting can cause us real stress, anxiety, or sadness. And that means they do matter to God.

The miracle at Cana shows that the Lord will sometimes intervene in very unexpected ways when we reach out to him. But even when he doesn't, he will help us put things in perspective and give us the comfort we need to get through, as any loving parent would do.

WHAT DO YOU THINK?

- Do you sometimes pray for small things? If you said no, do you worry the Lord doesn't want to get involved unless it's something really important? If you said yes, do you think praying for small things strengthens your relationship with the Lord?
- Are there any prayer requests that truly are improper to make to God?
- What do you think Jesus was thinking when his mother asked him to fix the wine shortage?

Chapter 38

THE WORLD'S GREATEST FISH STORY

(MATTHEW 4:18–22; MARK 1:16–20; LUKE 5:1–11; JOHN 1:35–51)

According to the book of Luke, Jesus was thirty years old when he began preaching, healing the sick, and performing his many other divine miracles (Luke 3:23). Biblical scholars believe his life on earth ended on the cross about three years later. Because Jesus knew he would not be around for long, assembling a select group of individuals to carry on his work after he died and ascended into heaven became a vital task. So he selected twelve men to be his apostles, including Simon, a fisherman who lived in Capernaum on the Sea of Galilee.

Soon after they met, Jesus changed Simon's name to Peter, which means "rock." Jesus explained this new name signified the important role that Peter would play in God's plan for salvation. Peter would serve as the foundation, like a strong and solid rock, for the new church that Jesus was creating. Peter participated in many of the most important days of Jesus' ministry and in the birth of the Christian church. So we are going to peek into Peter's thoughts and emotions, thanks to his "diary" entries in this and following chapters.

Obviously, these are not Peter's actual writings. But I constructed these entries around what Peter likely was thinking and feeling as the incredible story of Jesus' life unfolded before his very eyes. And I did so taking into full account what we do know from Scripture. The apostles were actual human beings with mixed emotions and motivations who didn't always understand what was happening. Recognizing their humanity and imagining what life must have been like for them can help us reconcile our own doubts and confusion and fears. So, let's look at how Peter describes the day he met Jesus.

Dear Diary,

Sorry for neglecting you the last few days, but there hasn't been much to write about. That is, until today.

Things started out pretty ordinary. We were out on the water well before dawn, and the sea was pretty calm. But the fish were nowhere to be found. I was so frustrated I started thinking I should have become a blacksmith like my mother wanted me to. Banging on hot metal all day isn't my idea of a good time, but at least I wouldn't have days like this when I work from sunup to sundown with nothing to show for it. I never would have guessed that such a bummer of a day could turn out so amazing!

After we gave up on trying to catch any fish and were back on shore, I noticed this guy talking to a bunch of people along the water's edge. He was a regular-looking guy, with regular-looking hair and beard. We were washing our nets, so I couldn't really hear what he was saying, but more and more people kept crowding around him. Eventually, he walked over to me and asked if I would take him out in my boat—just far enough from shore so he could speak to the crowd without getting crushed by the people.

At first I was annoyed. I was thinking, "Well, this guy has a lot of nerve. He's asking me to chauffeur him around on my boat for his fancy speaking engagement and not even offering to throw a little cash my way." But he seemed like a decent guy, so I figured, what the heck; I might as well do someone a good deed. So my brother, Andrew, and I got back on board and started rowing.

About fifty feet from shore, the guy told me to drop anchor, and then he went back to talking to the crowd. I got pretty interested in what he had to say about life and God. He told the crowd that in order to be truly happy and fulfilled, we need to stop thinking we are the center of the universe. Then we can surrender our lives to God and spend our time serving one another and being kind and loving. He talked for quite a while, but much of what he said boiled down to one thing: to save our lives, we have to be willing to give them up, to surrender to God and not spend so much time and effort trying to get ahead in the world. The one and only thing that will bring us real joy and meaning, he said, is living in God's light and doing his will. When he said that, it was like I suddenly understood why I've been feeling so empty for so long. I wasn't the only one. The crowd seemed to hang on his every word, like they were starving to death and his words were the food they were craving.

He finished by telling us that God understands us, inside and out, and that he even knows the exact number of hairs on our heads. I had always considered God to be a distant, ghost-like spirit who makes it rain and storm, and the sun rise and set—you know, the big stuff. But does he really know us? Does he pay attention to everyone and know all about us? Can I really have my own, personal connection to God? This guy was saying that God has a unique plan for each and every one of us, with a specific purpose in mind, tailored to our strengths and even our weaknesses. It made me feel, for the first time, that what I do here on earth really matters, in a forever kind of way.

It was weird, Diary. Even putting aside his amazing words, there was something about this guy that made me want to get to know him better. He was definitely smart, and he spoke with a lot of confidence. But I was most drawn to his kind and gentle spirit. He seemed more genuinely caring than anyone I ever met. By the time he finished talking, I figured out that this guy was Jesus, the man who was drawing crowds of people in the area who just wanted to hear him speak.

When he finished talking, Andrew and I got ready to row back to shore. But Jesus told me to pick up the anchor and take my boat out into deeper waters. So we did. When we got out pretty far, he told me to drop our nets. I explained that we had fished for hours and knew there were no fish to be found in that area. But he told us to do it anyway. So we did.

To my complete shock, our nets almost instantly became packed with fish. I had never seen anything like it. When the guys from the other boat saw us pulling in tons of fish, they quickly came out and dropped their nets too. Our two boats became so full that they practically sank. At first, all I could think about was how much money we were going to make from this enormous catch. But then it dawned on me that this whole thing with the fish was nothing short of a miracle. And if it was, this Jesus guy had to have come from God. That's when I started to get really scared.

I turned to Jesus, and he was looking directly at me. I felt like he could see deep into my soul, including all of my sins and the shame I've been carrying around for all of the bad things I've done. So I ran up to him and fell at his feet. "Go away from me, Jesus," I said. "I'm a sinful man." But Jesus just put his hand on my shoulder and said, "Don't be afraid. I have plans for you." I felt like a weight had been lifted off of me, and I could feel so much love flowing from every part of this man. I knew he was simply erasing my shame and my guilt.

Then he told me to follow him. Instead of being a fisherman, he told me I should be a "fisher for men" (Matt. 4:19). That sounds like a crazy thing to say, but I knew exactly what he meant. He was asking me to help open people's eyes to the truth, to tell them we need to stop sinning and being selfish in order to save our souls from a life of emptiness and despair. Jesus told me God wants me to help spread the good news. I realized that I had to decide whether I would continue living my life in the old way or leave it all behind and follow Jesus.

It didn't take me long to decide. When we got back to shore, I threw down my nets, left my fishing boat and the tons of fish right on the edge of the Sea of Galilee, and walked away with Jesus. And so did Andrew and our fishing buddies, James and John.

I don't know exactly what my life will bring from this day forward, but I trust this man, Jesus. I know for sure that my life will never be the same, and there's no turning back. Crazy, huh Diary?

In love and peace,
Simon Peter

WHAT DO YOU THINK?

- What was the significance of the miraculous number of fish Peter and the other fishermen caught?
- If you were Peter, would you have followed Jesus when he called you? Why or why not?
- Do you believe Jesus when he says the only path to true joy and fulfillment is to give up our old ways and surrender our lives to God? Why do you think more people don't follow that advice?

Chapter 39

YOUR OPTOMETRIST'S LEAST FAVORITE BIBLE TEACHING

(MATTHEW 5:27–30)

Early in his ministry, Jesus traveled with his disciples throughout Galilee, performing many miracles and preaching his message that salvation comes to those who surrender their lives to God and devote themselves to serving others in kindness, forgiveness, and love. Jesus also warned of the incredibly destructive power of sin. In his famous Sermon on the Mount, recorded in Matthew chapters 5 through 7, Jesus preached that sin can have a damaging and lasting impact on your soul and that you must do whatever it takes to free yourself from its crushing force over your life. He told his listeners:

> If your right eye causes you to stumble, pluck it out and throw it away from you. … If your right hand causes you to stumble, cut it off, and throw it away from you. For it is more profitable for you that one of your members should perish, than for your whole body to be cast into [hell] (Matt. 5:29–30).

Well, that's kind of harsh, don't you think?

But, obviously, Jesus wasn't telling people to literally pluck out their eyeballs or dismember themselves. *That* would be crazy … Instead, he was using extreme language to make a very important point: our lives here on earth, in addition to being imperfect, are temporary. Compared to the afterlife, which goes on forever and ever, our earthly lives are just a flash in time, like the blink of an eye. So indulging sinful desires, even if it brings us momentary pleasure, isn't worth risking the loss of eternal happiness in the Kingdom of Heaven.

Even though God forgives us for messing up here on earth, it's possible to get so swallowed up in sin that your life becomes like a runaway train heading farther and farther away from God. Sometimes sin so profoundly devastates your very soul that it's almost impossible to turn back.

If Jesus isn't really asking us to damage our bodies, what kind of action is he talking about? Well, it might be ending a relationship with your best friend since kindergarten because you know he is leading you down a dangerous road away from God. Or it could be unfollowing your favorite Instagram influencer because you realize that person's lifestyle is causing you to focus too much on image and material things.

Cutting off a friend or changing your media habits or other deeply ingrained behaviors can sometimes feel like you're severing a part of you. But it may be the only way to avoid slipping down a deadly path. Jesus tells us it's better to lose a limb than have your whole body cast into hell. Although he's not telling us to physically dismember parts of our body, he is warning us that extreme danger requires extreme actions. And his words of caution should be heeded.

WHAT DO YOU THINK?

- I gave you a couple of examples of what "plucking out your eye" might mean in our real lives. What are other examples?

- How can you know when it's time to cut off a relationship with someone who is too immersed in a life of sin? What steps should you take to end the relationship?

- Other than Jesus, everyone who ever lived has sinned. Where does the desire to sin come from?

- Do you believe it's possible to completely stop sinning? If not, then why even try?

Chapter 40

OUCH! DOUBLE OUCH!
(MATTHEW 5:38–42; LUKE 6:27–31)

When someone slaps you in the face, turn your head and offer the other cheek, too. And if someone wants to take the shirt off your back, give it to them, and then offer your jacket, too.

No, these are not my ideas—they are the words of Jesus in Matthew 5:39–40. And as a father, I can tell you that I did not pass along these words to my kids as literal commands. We began teaching our kids when they were very young to be respectful and kind to everyone. However, we also taught them to stand up for themselves and not let anyone take advantage of them or treat them badly. And, in my heart, I believe that Jesus was listening to those lessons with approval.

So what about this whole "turn the other cheek" thing? Was Jesus giving us practical advice on how to respond when someone physically assaults us?

Step 1. Get slapped by some jerk.

Step 2. Shed a few tears.

Step 3. Turn your head about forty-five degrees the other way to make it easy for said jerk to slap you from the other direction.

Step 4. Get slapped again.

Step 5. Cry a bit harder because now both sides of your face hurt.

Step 6. Shake hands with the perpetrator and complete the transaction.

Of course that's not what Jesus was talking about! He was using exaggerated language to drive home a simple point: when someone is angry and wants to engage in some serious mud-slinging, we need to take the high road. We are all born into this world with a survival instinct and, for most of us, our brains respond to aggression with more aggression.

Jesus says we need to reprogram the way we think about our fellow human beings. We must stop responding to anger with even more anger. It's not our job to even the score or ensure that everyone gets what they deserve. God will take care of that.

Instead, we need to be kind and caring to everyone, even to the people who are unkind to us. God didn't send his one and only son to earth just to make sure we brush our teeth, say our prayers, and help little old ladies across the street. Jesus came here for a purpose much greater than that. He came to change our hearts and minds, and his message was revolutionary. He said we should no longer reserve the love in our hearts for the people close to us, like our parents, siblings, or best friends. Instead, we need to love everyone, even our enemies, because we're all children of God.

So how do we apply Jesus' teaching to our own lives? In the real world, most of us don't go around slapping each other. So Jesus probably wasn't talking about the playground bully threatening to punch you in the nose if you don't surrender your lunch money—although he does expect you to love that person too. These verses help us understand how we should react to the verbal power plays, criticisms, or personal affronts that we all encounter, often from the people close to us. According to the world's rules, when this happens, we should create some serious drama and show the other guy who is boss. Just watch one hour of reality TV. Mean and nasty tirades are not only tolerated, but glorified.

Jesus is saying, when you are confronted in this way, rise above the anger and treat the other person with kindness and, dare I say it, love. Yes, love. If you do, you will be demonstrating the strength and courage that come from making God the master of your life. On the other hand, if you let people drag you down into the muck, you may never mature beyond the level of a child or know how it feels to live honorably and earn the respect of those around you.

If you have any doubt about it, try this challenge. The next time someone slings some verbal cow-poop in your face, be the bigger person and take the high road, whatever that means in the situation. Afterward, compare how you feel to how you felt the last time you got into a nasty war of words with someone. I guarantee, you'll find that "turning the other cheek" is sound advice for feeling good about yourself. It also might help others see the goodness that shines from living Christ's way and open their hearts to following God and living in his light. Jesus' instruction that we turn the other cheek and love everyone, even our enemies, requires nothing less.

WHAT DO YOU THINK?

- Think about a time when you got into a heated argument with someone else and said some really mean things. How did you feel afterward?
- Think about someone you know who typically remains calm and collected even when confronted by an angry person. Would you describe that person as strong or weak?
- Jesus taught us: "Don't be afraid of those who kill the body, but are not able to kill the soul. Rather, fear him who is able to destroy both soul and body" (Matt. 10:28). How does turning the other cheek keep us from letting someone "destroy our souls"?
- What would you do if you discovered that someone in your social circle is trashing you to your friends behind your back? How would Jesus want you to handle that situation?

Chapter 41

DON'T MIND ME; I'M JUST DROPPING IN FOR A QUICK MIRACLE

(MATTHEW 9:1–8; MARK 2:1–12; LUKE 5:17–26)

How far would you go to help a friend? Would you lay down your life for that person? Would you risk making a public spectacle out of yourself while trying to save them from a horrible fate? Well, in Jesus' day, four men who wanted to help their paralyzed buddy had to face the public spectacle question. And they answered with a resounding "yes!"

Our story begins with Jesus preaching to a crowd of people, as he often did. However, on this day, he wasn't preaching on a hillside, at the edge of the sea, or in a temple. Instead, he was inside an ordinary house in the town of Capernaum. And, by this point, so many had heard the news about Jesus, his incredible message, and the many miracles he was performing that huge crowds were following him wherever he went. In fact, the home in which he was preaching was so packed that the people were spilling out into the streets.

The heroes of our story heard about Jesus and his incredible power to heal the sick. They wanted more than anything to get

Jesus to heal their paralytic friend. Because the man couldn't sit up, his friends had to carry him around, flat on his back, on a mat. Knowing they couldn't even get close to the front door, the guys had to devise a plan to somehow get their friend in front of Jesus.

So, while Jesus was preaching, they climbed onto the roof with their buddy and began a mini-demolition project, cutting a large hole in the roof. When they were done, they lowered their friend into the room right in front of Jesus.

Now, if any of us regular human beings were standing in Jesus' shoes—or, more accurately, Jesus' sandals—at that moment, we probably would have screamed something like: "You idiots! You got chunks of roof on my head! What are you trying to do, kill me? And you just interrupted my story about the time I healed five demon-possessed men and fourteen lepers all in one day. RUDE!"

But that's why God didn't appoint us as the Lord and Savior of all humanity. Jesus, being who he is, instead was impressed at the incredible faith these men showed and their devotion to their friend. However, Jesus didn't heal the paralyzed man right away. Instead, he looked straight at the paralyzed man and told him: "Son, your sins are forgiven you" (Mark 2:5).

The Jewish leaders in the room were shocked by Jesus' words. They thought, "Wow, this Jesus dude must think an awful lot of himself. Only God can forgive sins, so he must think HE is God!" Jesus, actually being the Lord himself, knew exactly what they were thinking. So he called them on it. He said something to the effect of, "Yep, saying I forgive sins is a huge deal. But to prove to you that I have this authority, I'm going to work a miracle, right here and now." He then commanded the paralyzed man to stand up, pick up his mat, and go home. And that's what he did.

The men who brought their friend to Jesus demonstrated the incredible power of faith and love. But their actions also present a challenge to every one of us. We all like to think we would do whatever it takes to rescue someone we care about who desperately needs our help. Almost all of us would give up a Saturday afternoon to sit with a friend who is in the hospital. Or we'd drop everything to watch our neighbors' kids if they had to deal with some personal emergency. We might even cough up some money for a close friend who truly needs a financial lifeline. But what about openly professing belief in Jesus? Would you take that action if you thought that doing so might save a friend or loved one from a horrible fate? A lot of us just aren't willing to go that far.

Let's face it, we all want to be cool. And publicly displaying our commitment to God probably isn't going to win us a seat at the cool kids' table in the high school cafeteria. I'm not talking about making a public spectacle of yourself and exhibiting your faith to the entire world. But even sharing with a friend what God has done in your life can sometimes be uncomfortable. Recognize, however, that if you care about someone whose life has gone completely off the rails, just telling your story about your relationship with God might help turn them to the Lord and rescue them from a life of hopelessness and self-destruction.

So, ask yourself, when someone you love desperately needs God in their life, will you care enough to do what it takes? Will your love be strong enough to get you past your fear and discomfort so you can profess your faith, which might be the best hope for rescuing your friend from their current mess? If you have not faced a moment like this yet, trust me, it will come. That's why I'm encouraging you to think about it now.

At least one group of guys rose to that challenge to bring their friend to Jesus. They ignored their fear of looking crazy, angering a huge crowd, or getting sued for destroying someone's property to dangle their paralytic friend from a hole in a roof—an expression of strength, bravery, and love. They showed the world what's possible when you have both faith in the Lord and boundless love in your heart. Now THAT is cool.

WHAT DO YOU THINK?

- Have you ever asked others to pray for a friend or family member who was sick or in trouble? If not, why not? If yes, how did it make you feel?
- To what extent have you publicly professed your faith? Do your nonreligious friends know you're a Christian? If not, what is preventing you from telling them?
- If the four men in our story simply had prayed to God to heal their friend instead of carrying him to Jesus, do you think the man would have been healed anyway?

Chapter 42

THE NOTORIOUS SABBATH GRAIN SCANDAL

(MATTHEW 12:1–14; MARK 2:23–28; 3:1–6; LUKE 6:1–11)

One Saturday Jesus was traveling through a grain field, and his disciples were hungry. You never knew when Jesus might decide to stop and eat, so the disciples began picking some heads of grain off the stalks and eating them. Some Pharisees—the religious leaders who specialized in interpreting Jewish law—criticized Jesus for how his disciples were feeding themselves.

By this time in Jesus' ministry, he was gaining quite a following with the Jewish people. And the religious leaders were feeling threatened. They worried that they would lose power if all the people started following Jesus, so they began looking for chances to make Jesus look bad in front of his followers.

According to Jewish law, if a person was hungry, they were allowed to eat the grain from someone else's field as long as they didn't use any tools to harvest it, ate only enough to satisfy their hunger, and didn't carry any away with them. The disciples had followed those commands, but the Pharisees were complaining because they had done it on the Sabbath. Remember those Ten Commandments that God handed over to Moses, way back in the wilderness? Well, the fourth one says,

> *Remember the Sabbath day, to keep it holy. You shall labor six days, and do all your work, but the seventh day is a Sabbath to Yahweh your God. You shall not do any work in it ... for in six days Yahweh made heaven and earth, the sea, and all that is in them, and rested the seventh day; therefore Yahweh blessed the Sabbath day, and made it holy* (Exod. 20:8–11).

The Pharisees argued that picking grain, rubbing it between your hands to separate the wheat from the chaff, and eating it was "work," and therefore the disciples were breaking the Sabbath rules. Jesus defended his disciples, not by arguing that picking grain didn't qualify as work, but by suggesting that the Pharisees were missing the point.

Jesus reminded the Pharisees that David had done something similar before he became king of Israel. Like Jesus' disciples, David's men were hungry, so he convinced the Jewish high priest to give them five loaves of bread that, according to Jewish law, could be eaten only by Jewish priests. Jesus exposed the hypocrisy of the Pharisees by bringing up David, an honored and revered figure from Jewish history. He asked why they had never criticized David's action, which was a much more serious breach of Jewish law than plucking some wheat off a stalk and eating it.

The Pharisees didn't quite know how to answer Jesus about that, so they just tagged along when he went to pray in the synagogue, a Jewish house of worship. Taking another crack at tripping up Jesus, the Pharisees pointed to a man with a shriveled hand and asked if it was "lawful to heal on the Sabbath day" (Matt. 12:10). They knew that Jesus frequently healed sick or injured people, but healing might qualify as "work," which would be another violation of the fourth commandment.

Jesus answered their question with a question. "If you have a sheep that falls into a sinkhole on the Sabbath, would you pull it out?" The Pharisees didn't want to answer Jesus. He waited until the silence got uncomfortable and then said, "Since people are more valuable than animals, I say it's okay to do a good deed on the Sabbath." Then Jesus told the man with the shriveled hand to stretch it out, and his hand was fully healed.

Through his examples, explanations, and actions, Jesus demonstrated that the Pharisees had no leg to stand on, and this made them really angry. In essence, Jesus was saying that the Pharisees, who were charged with interpreting Jewish law, were missing the whole point of why the laws and religious rules existed in the first place.

Quoting from the book of Hosea, Jesus told the Pharisees that they should understand that God desires "mercy, and not sacrifice," and to stop condemning "the guiltless" (Matt. 12:7). In other words, God's highest calling is not for his people to strictly follow the letter of every religious law or rule. Instead, his greatest wish is for his people to be kind and merciful and care for those in need. That doesn't mean the Ten Commandments or other religious laws, rules, or holy traditions are not important. They are. But they need to be put in perspective.

I grew up in the Greek Orthodox Church, and one of our holy traditions was to fast for several days before we took Holy

Communion. We also fasted during the week before Easter. The fast did not require us to go without all food, but to give up meat, dairy products, and foods made with vegetable or olive oil. Back in those days, there weren't a lot of appetizing vegetarian or vegan food options, and, honestly, my mom wasn't particularly good with the options we had. So our fasting time was pretty unpleasant.

One of our staples during our fasts was *fakes*, a Greek lentil soup that tasted like mud. When I complained, my mother suggested I jazz it up with vinegar. That only made the fakes taste like mud cooked inside a sweaty gym sock. Another favorite in my mom's repertoire of fasting-friendly treats was lettuce, tomato, and mustard sandwiches. Obviously, this option was missing a main ingredient. "Hello? Can we have at least a slice of salami or two?" But every Greek kid's worst nightmare was *spanakorizo*: rice, spinach, and tomato sauce all mushed together into one nauseating pile of gruel.

I thought fasting was just one more thing dreamed up by adults to torture kids. Why? Because they could. But as I got older, I realized giving up some of our favorite foods for a little while was a way of showing our gratitude to God. Fasting also breaks up our normal routine and helps put us in a reflective mindset, so in the days before Easter and Holy Communion we could pay more attention to matters of the spirit instead of cheeseburgers, pizza, or Twinkies.

Fasting, like many religious rules and traditions, is important because it's an action we can take to demonstrate our devotion and obedience to our Creator by actively participating in a rich religious tradition that glorifies God. And participating in these sorts of practices with other people keeps us connected to a Christian community.

My mother and father believed fasting was important for all of these reasons. But if one of us got sick during a fast, my mother would ditch the fakes and the spanakorizo and prepare a big pot of chicken soup. (In the interest of full disclosure, it was Greek chicken soup called *avgolemono*, with rice and a creamy egg and lemon mixture. It was absolutely delicious and the perfect comfort food.) Although my parents strongly believed in following the fasting requirements, they also knew those rules were sometimes meant to be broken. They knew God is more concerned about caring for a sick child than following rules for a seasonal fast.

My guess is that the Pharisees also understood that the Jewish religious laws had to be applied with some measure of balance, concern for others, and common sense. But they were more interested in discrediting Jesus than looking for balance. When Jesus outfoxed them and exposed them for the hypocrites that they were, the Pharisees were furious. Matthew tells us that after Jesus healed the man with the withered hand, the Pharisees went out and "conspired against him," looking for ways to "destroy him" (Matt. 12:14).

WHAT DO YOU THINK?

- Why did the Jewish leaders feel so threatened by Jesus?
- The fourth commandment told the Jewish people to remember the Sabbath day (Saturday) to keep it holy. Most Christians believe this commandment today means we should attend church on Sundays to worship with other believers. Do you believe that? Is there some flexibility in that requirement? Where do you draw the line between allowing yourself some flexibility and knowing when you're breaking the commandment?
- In your own faith, which religious rules or traditions do you feel are most important? Which ones do you wish didn't exist?
- What would it be like if there were no rules or religious traditions at all?
- Have you ever caught yourself judging someone in your church or faith group for violating a religious "rule"? Did you say something to the person? Did you talk about that person's behavior to someone else?

Chapter 43

RIGHTEOUS CROWDS, WRETCHED SOULS

(JOHN 8:1–11)

We often judge others by a much tougher standard than we apply to ourselves. That's the lesson Jesus taught in a memorable way to Jewish leaders who brought him a woman accused of a sin that supposedly was deserving of the death penalty.

Jesus was preaching in the temple in Jerusalem when a group of Pharisees and other Jewish leaders noisily interrupted. They pushed through all the people who were listening to Jesus, dragging a distraught woman with them. They shoved the woman into the space around Jesus and said she was guilty of adultery, which means she had been having intimate relations with someone who was not her husband.

"What should we do with her?" the Jewish leaders asked Jesus. "Remember that the law of Moses says she should be stoned." These men were willing to start the stoning, a brutal form of execution, then and there. But they wanted Jesus to give the command.

You see, the Pharisees were up to their usual tricks trying to get Jesus in trouble with the Jewish people. If Jesus said, "Stone her," he would probably lose favor with the people who believed killing the woman would be overly harsh and cruel. However, if Jesus said, "Let her go," then the Jewish leaders could accuse him of rejecting the religious laws.

But Jesus outsmarted them with the perfect answer. He said, "He who is without sin among you, let him throw the first stone at her" (John 8:7). After he said that, Jesus stooped down and doodled in the dirt, not watching what the men were doing. But Jesus' words were obviously ringing in their ears. One by one, they simply walked away, until the only people left were Jesus and the woman. Jesus stood up then and faced the woman.

> *"Woman, where are your accusers? Did no one condemn you?"*
>   *She said, "No one, Lord."*
>   *Jesus said, "Neither do I condemn you. Go your way. From now on, sin no more" (John 8:10–11).*

Jesus knew the woman was a sinner. And he knew all of her accusers were also sinners and not really in a great position to judge or condemn her. Only one person in that group was without sin, but Jesus chose to offer mercy instead of condemnation, encouragement instead of punishment.

It's easy for us to get fired up and feel good about ourselves when we focus on bad things other people are doing. However, when we're honest with ourselves, we have to admit we're all guilty of some pretty bad stuff, especially when you consider the things other people can't see, like what's going on inside of our minds and hearts. Jesus drove this point home in how he worded his challenge to the men in this incident. He didn't say, "Okay, those of you without sin can throw the rocks." Knowing humans find safety in numbers, he wasn't going to let any of them pretend to be blameless while going along with the crowd. Jesus would not let one rock be thrown unless and until one of them stepped up and publicly claimed he was without sin. Jesus knew none of them could meet that challenge. We are all sinners, after all.

In Matthew, Jesus said, "Don't judge, so that you won't be judged" (Matt. 7:1). He then asked why we try to remove a speck of sawdust from our brother's eye when we have a log in our own eye. In other words, why are you noticing the little things someone else does wrong and overlooking your own huge mistakes?

God sees inside us and knows we carry around resentment, selfish pride, jealousy, greed, and other sins of the heart that affect our choices and how we treat each other. Let's not be hypocrites and pretend otherwise. Remember, when you cast stones at your neighbors, God will judge you as harshly as you judge others.

WHAT DO YOU THINK?

- Crowds are capable of committing brutal acts that a person would be far less likely to do on their own. In addition to forcing the men in this story to reflect on their own sins, how did Jesus' actions work to save the woman's life?
- Do you think most people portray themselves differently in public versus how they view themselves in the quiet of their own rooms?
- The Bible teaches us not to judge others because that's the Lord's job. But does that mean we can't "judge" or reject behavior that goes against Christian teaching? How do we recognize the difference?
- What is the right way to respond to destructive or sinful behavior in others?

Chapter 44

ALL THOSE DANCING LESSONS FINALLY PAID OFF!

(MATTHEW 14:1–12; MARK 6:12–29; LUKE 9:7–9)

Remember John the Baptist? Jesus' cousin who ate locusts and baptized Jesus? Well, let me introduce you to the characters involved with John's final days. You'll see, this crew could have come straight out of a trashy novel.

First, there's the rich and powerful King Herod, who ruled over Galilee and was the son of Herod the Great. Next, there was Herodias. She was both Herod's wife and his ex-sister-in-law. (Yep, you read that right—more about that later.) She wins the prize for the most wickedly evil character in our story, but she had some stiff competition. Then there's Herodias' daughter from her first marriage to Herod's brother. The Bible doesn't identify her by name, so we'll just call her Twinkle-Toes. (Keep reading and you'll find out why.)

John the Baptist was doing what he was put on earth to do: preach to the people and tell them to repent and stop sinning. He was a tough-minded, no-nonsense Baptist, so he had no qualms about throwing a bucket of cold water on people's good times if necessary. And one of John's cold-water buckets had Herod's name written all over it.

You see, Herod had fallen for Herodias, the wife of his half-brother, Philip. So Herod ditched his own wife and swept Herodias off her feet—and away from Philip. And John wasn't the kind of preacher who would keep his mouth shut in the face of such unabashed sleaze. He told Herod to knock off the funny business with Herodias and repent. So Herod did what any self-respecting, power-hungry despot would do: he threw John in jail. There, no one could hear John scream about Herod's sins. Now, Herodias was even more upset than Herod about John's criticisms of their power-couple status. And she thought prison wasn't punishment enough for John. She wanted him dead. But Herod knew John was a righteous man, so he wanted to keep John safe, but silenced, in prison.

So that's where things stood when Herod threw a birthday bash for himself and invited all of his top public officials, military commanders, and other bigwigs. At the height of the party, after Herod likely had fallen head-first into the wine bottle (in other words, was pretty schnookered), Herodias sent in her daughter, Twinkle-Toes, to dance for the king. And did she ever dance! She shimmied, she pranced, she skipped and dipped and twirled like a whirling dervish on steroids. Twinkle-Toes shook her booty and cut the rug like nobody had ever seen before. At the end of her performance, she leapt across the dance floor like a gazelle in her final Grand Jeté, and the crowd erupted in cheers!

King Herod, in all of his alcohol-fueled exuberance, jumped to his feet, so overwhelmed by Twinkle-Toes' performance that he was ready to make a rash promise. "Ask me whatever you want, and I will give it to you … Whatever you shall ask of me, I will give you, up to half of my kingdom" (Mark 6:22–23).

Twinkle-Toes, recognizing this was the opportunity of a lifetime, wasn't going to squander it by jumping into a hasty decision. So she ran to her mother for advice on what her big ask should be. Her mother didn't hesitate: "The head of John the [Baptist]," she told her daughter (Mark 6:24).

No doubt, Twinkle-Toes responded something to the effect of: "Are you crazy? I can have anything in the whole wide world and you want me to ask for some guy's bloody noggin on a platter? Everyone in this God-forsaken kingdom knows you're a wicked she-devil in designer clothes. But this crosses the line even for you, old lady."

And Herodias' response? She assuredly wasn't going to let Twinkle-Toes have the last word: "You listen to me, you overrated little diva. If you think I hatched this ingenious, albeit evil, plan just so you could score a quick pile of cash from your idiot stepfather, and possibly get a spot on the next season of *Jerusalem's Got Talent*, you are sadly mistaken. Now do as I say or I'll make sure that your next flying leap will be off the cliffs of Mount Sinai!"

Not wanting to be the next pile of purple and pink bedazzled roadkill at the bottom of a mountain, Twinkle-Toes dutifully complied. She sashayed back into the banquet room and told Herod, "I want you to give me right now the head of John the [Baptist] on a platter" (Mark 6:25).

Herod immediately knew he had been outsmarted. "Wow. I expected her to ask for her own royal palace, or maybe a handsome prince. But John's head? My darling wife must have put her up to this." Herod didn't really want to slaughter John, but he couldn't back out of the promise he had made in front of the entire party crowd. So he sent some guards to take care of it, and it wasn't long before they delivered John's head on a platter to Twinkle-Toes, who passed it on to her mother.

The death of John the Baptist reveals the immense power of evil in our world and how far some people will go to silence the voice of righteousness. John was a good man who simply couldn't sit by silently in the face of the morally bankrupt behavior of Herod and Herodias. When John told them that they were committing a grave sin against God, their spouses, and each other, it was like he was holding up a mirror, forcing them to see themselves and their actions in the clear light of day. And they couldn't bear that view. But instead of seeking God's forgiveness and changing their behavior, Herod threw John in jail and Herodias devised her horrific plan to kill God's messenger.

Unfortunately, the Herods and Herodiases of the world have always existed and are still present in our world. These people are so steeped in sin and depravity that they go into attack mode when they are confronted by someone whose honorable behavior casts light on their own bad conduct. But thank God for the John-the-Baptists of the world. These fearless and tough-as-nails Christians won't back down from the bad guys and are ready to accept their earthly consequences, knowing their eternal safety is in God's hands.

The question for each of us: do we have that strength and courage to stand up and defend our Christian values—values like kindness, love, and morality—even when we might attract the wrath of ungodly wrongdoers? If we do, we can take comfort in knowing that the Lord will be fighting the good fight with us and will ensure that we prevail in the end. We also will gain the respect of those around us and establish ourselves as a leader among our peers, a great feeling for sure. And, beyond the immediate rewards for standing firm in our beliefs, the spiritual rewards will be both unlimited and eternal.

WHAT DO YOU THINK?

- John the Baptist had a very direct and confrontational style of preaching. Do you think there's a place for that style in today's world? Do you think it could be effective in some circumstances?
- Why do you think Herodias could not just ignore John the Baptist? Why did she resort to such extreme actions?
- Have you ever seen people today lash out at the righteous in an effort to silence them?
- What stops us from standing up and fighting against sin and evil in our lives and in our world?

Chapter 45

DOES ANYONE HAVE 10,000 PLASTIC FORKS THEY CAN SPARE?

(MATTHEW 14:13–36; MARK 6:30–56; LUKE 9:10–17; JOHN 6:1–24)

Dear Diary,

These days, life is going a million miles a minute. In fact, there's so much going on, it's hard for me to keep it all straight in my head. The news about Jesus has spread like wildfire, so the crowds have been surrounding us practically 24/7. Even when we try to get some one-on-one time with him, sooner or later, they find us. Yesterday was a perfect example.

When Jesus heard the horrible news about John the Baptist, he asked us to get the boat ready so we could push off to a new place. He wanted to find a secluded spot along the water's edge where we could regroup and spend some alone time. But there was already a crowd waiting for us when we got to shore. To be honest, I was hoping Jesus would send them away. No such luck. He welcomed them, started healing the sick people, and then told everyone how to live a life full of love and service. Very quickly, the crowd grew, and before we knew it, there were about 5,000 men there! Plus, about the same number of women and children.

After a few hours, some of us apostles started worrying about dinner time. We gently suggested to Jesus that it was time to send the crowd on their merry way. But Jesus being Jesus, he wouldn't hear of it. He told us to give dinner to the crowd. We were like, excuse me? We have exactly five loaves of bread and two fish among us. And there are THOUSANDS of hungry people here. So unless God was planning another manna and quail drop à la Moses in the desert, the dinner thing just wasn't happening. But Jesus said there would be more than enough and asked us to bring the fish and bread to him. Of course, we did as he asked.

He said a prayer of thanksgiving over the food and then told us to distribute it to the people. I was thinking, maybe Jesus wanted us to give everyone a crumb of bread and one speck of fish, so we could say we "fed" them. But here's the crazy part: every time we took a loaf of bread or piece of fish off the tray, another one appeared. This went on for over an hour. By that point in the evening, the people were so hungry they ate like total pigs. But there was still a ton of food left over. When they were done, we gathered up twelve baskets full of extra bread and fish!

After all that, we were exhausted. So we again asked Jesus if we could tell these people to scram. Jesus said he would take care of that, but he wanted us to get in the boat and set sail toward the town of Gennesaret. I was thinking: "That's weird, isn't he coming with us? How's he going to get there?" But after the bread-and-fish miracle, I was pretty sure he could manage his own transportation. So we got in the boat and pushed off from shore. Once we were out pretty far, the winds started to kick up. Before long, we were getting tossed around like a toy boat. The wind got so fierce and the seas got so rough that we thought for sure we were going to die. Needless to say, none of us could sleep. We kept looking for signs that the storm would calm down, but it just wasn't letting up.

Next thing we knew, out of the darkness, we saw what looked like a ghost standing on top of the raging waters. And it was heading toward our boat! It was terrifying! But as it got closer, we could see that it wasn't a ghost at all, it was Jesus. I was so relieved to see him, I just wanted to run up to him and give him a big bear-hug. I don't know what came over me, but I yelled to him and asked if I could walk out onto the water, just like he was doing, so I could be with him right in that moment. He was like, "Sure thing, come on!"

So I climbed over the side of the boat and jumped down onto the water. And I didn't sink. At first, I wasn't even thinking about the huge waves and ferocious winds. I just kept looking at Jesus and chugging along toward him. But as I got closer to him, I looked around and then got distracted. I thought: "Oh my gosh! I'm standing here on top of a raging sea in the middle of a typhoon. I'm going to drown!" And THAT'S when I started to sink!

I hollered for Jesus to help me, and he reached out and grabbed my hand. "Oh, Peter," he said. "Why did you doubt me? Your faith is still pretty weak, isn't it?"

I didn't answer him at the time but, looking back, I see that I began doubting the instant I took my eyes off of Jesus. This is a lesson I need to remember. As long as I fix my sights on Jesus and trust him, he'll help me overcome whatever challenges come my way. Of course, that sounds easy now. But it wasn't so easy when the winds were yanking on my clothes and the waves were smacking me in the knees and spraying water all over my face. But I know I can't let myself get sidetracked and lose sight of Jesus, because he's my lifeline to a safe place in the storm. I'll always remember today and know that, when I find myself sinking, I just need to look for Jesus.

Anyway, after Jesus and I walked together back to the boat, the sea calmed down. We made it to Gennesaret by late morning, where we were greeted by more crowds, of course. More crazy stuff happened there, but I have to save that for another day. I can't keep my eyes open.

Before I hit the sack, I gotta say this for the record: although this life is pretty exhausting and filled with drama, I feel so grateful that Jesus picked me to be one of his apostles. I'll never regret my decision to follow him, not for one moment.

In love and peace,
Peter

WHAT DO YOU THINK?

- The crowds who had come to Jesus probably had plenty of food waiting for them at home. So why did Jesus want to feed them? Why would he use his miraculous powers for something as trivial as providing dinner?
- In the middle of the storms in our lives, what are some ways we can keep our eyes fixed on Jesus?
- During times of personal crises, how do we know when to simply trust in God and when to take action?

Chapter 46

LOVE BEYOND YOUR FRIEND GROUP

(LUKE 10:25–37)

Being kind to your best friend is easy. Let's face it, you enjoy doing the same things, probably laugh at the same jokes, and feel like you just "get" each other. You never really mind going out of your way to help out your best buddies. In fact, it probably makes you feel good.

But how do you treat the kids in your class who have really annoying personalities? Are you nice to the girl who, in high school, still has pictures of the Disney Princesses hung inside her locker? Or what about the guy who sits next to you in math class—the one who smells like hard-boiled eggs? Are you as kind to them as you are to your best friends? Well, if you're like most people, probably not.

The Jewish leaders in Jesus' day knew they were supposed to "love their neighbors" as much as they loved themselves, but they also knew that wasn't easy to do. The Jewish people were very good to their own families and other Jews, but they weren't always very nice to people they saw as "outsiders." They were anything but friendly to the Romans, and they had a centuries-long feud going with the Samaritans, a religious and ethnic group who lived in the region.

So one day, a Jewish scholar asked Jesus about that "neighbor" part of the command. "Who is my neighbor, anyway?" Instead of answering directly, Jesus told a story.

"Once upon a time," Jesus said, "a Jewish man was walking from Jerusalem to Jericho when some thieves attacked him, beat him up, and took everything he had, including all his clothes. They then left him to die on the side of the road. Not too long after the robbers took off, a Jewish priest came by. He saw the man, but just kept walking. A little while later, another Jewish man came by. He also just walked on by, pretending not to see the guy lying there bleeding and moaning. Finally, a Samaritan man came along. He saw the half-dead, naked guy and stopped to help. The Samaritan bandaged up the victim as best he could, then loaded him up onto his donkey and took him to an inn. The Samaritan paid for the man's room and left money so he could get all the healthcare he needed."

Jesus finished his story and then turned back to the Jewish scholar. "Now which of these three do you think seemed to be a neighbor to him who fell among the robbers?" (Luke 10:36). "The one who showed mercy," the Jewish leader answered. Then "go and do likewise," Jesus said (Luke 10:37). There are so many lessons you can pull out of this story, but I want to focus on two of them.

First, as people of God, we need to help others who are in need, even when it's not convenient. In Jesus' story, the first guy to walk past the man in great need was a priest: someone who is supposed to help people in need. No doubt, the priest had a great excuse for why he couldn't stop that particular day.

We can always come up with some legitimate reason for not helping out: "Gee, I hope someone stops to help that kid who just wiped out on his bike. I would stop, I really would, but I have to get to class. I can't get another tardy. Besides, what can I do anyway? It would be better if some grown-up stopped so they could take him home or wherever."

You get the point. We all have busy lives and there's always a great excuse for letting someone else step in when a poor soul needs our help. But God calls us to have a kind and loving spirit. And that sometimes means we have to perform an act of kindness even when we don't feel like it. Or even if we might have to face the consequences for our third tardy of the month.

The second point of this story is that we need to be kind to everyone, not just members of our own crowd. The good guy in our story didn't let the prejudices that Samaritans and Jews had for one another stop him from showing love for the man who was robbed and beaten. This lesson was brought home to me personally one New Year's Eve, not long after I moved to Boston. I was invited to accompany a friend to a party in one of the city's most upscale neighborhoods. I was new in town and didn't know many people, so I gladly accepted. But when we arrived at the party, I noticed two things that immediately made me feel awkward and insecure.

First, most people at the party were decked out in really nice clothes. The women wore fancy cocktail dresses, and the men wore suits. My friend and I were the only guests wearing jeans and sweaters, so I felt kind of grubby. Plus, we were the only white people at the party. Everyone else was African American. I would not have expected that to bother me but, truth be told, I felt like an intruder when I walked into that party. I worried that the host and hostess might not really want me there because we had never met and because I was such a visible outsider.

But after I met the other party-goers, I realized my concerns were just a product of my own hang-ups and insecurities. The host, hostess, and everyone at the party weren't just polite and cordial. They went out of their way to introduce themselves to me and make me feel comfortable. Everyone was so warm and friendly that I forgot I looked different, not to mention underdressed. Then I realized that most of the party guests had probably been to dozens of parties where they were the only ones with a different skin color. The warm welcome they extended to my friend and me humbled me and made me wonder whether I had extended that same extra level of kindness and attentiveness in the past when the tables were turned. I regret having to say, probably not.

All of this brings us back to the question the Jewish scholar asked Jesus: who is our "neighbor"? The answer? *Everyone* is our neighbor. We must extend the same kindness to strangers, people outside our social circles, and folks we may not like very much as we do to our family and best friends. The story of the Good Samaritan reminds us that we are all God's children and therefore deserve each other's respect, compassion, and love.

WHAT DO YOU THINK?

- Has a stranger ever helped you out of a predicament? Why do you think they helped you?
- The Bible tells us to love everyone, even our enemies. Is that possible? What does "love" mean in this context?
- When you see someone who could use help, do you get involved? How do you make your decision about whether or not to assist?
- When you treat someone with kindness, you are following God's command. Are there other benefits to acting that way?

Chapter 47

THE SPIRITUAL PRICE OF A SPOTLESS KITCHEN

(LUKE 10:38–42)

It's hard to picture Jesus as having real friends. His mission here on earth—to save the souls of all of humanity—was so monumental that it's no wonder we think of him as a pretty serious guy. And most of the stories about him in the Bible describe Jesus preaching, healing the sick, and fending off those nasty Pharisees. So who had time for socializing? The disciples seemed to genuinely like Jesus, and they certainly spent a lot of time with him. But they also called him "Teacher" and "Master" and "Lord," so it's hard to envision them as Jesus' true besties. It just wasn't that kind of relationship.

But of course, Jesus must have had a lot of friends. He was human after all. And also loving, kind, and wise. In fact, the Bible tells us about three of his closest buddies, who happened to be siblings. Their names were Martha, Mary, and Lazarus. One afternoon, the two sisters were expecting Jesus to visit them at their home. Martha was clearly the uptight one, probably the older sister, and Mary was the chill one of the duo. Martha was doing her typical big-sister thing: scrubbing the floors, dusting the furniture, and probably making one heck of a tuna casserole.

After Jesus arrived, Martha continued running around the house doing her best hostess-with-the-mostess routine. Mary, on the other hand, was sitting at Jesus' feet listening to him preach. So Martha did what any respectable big sister would do: she ratted out her lazy little sister to Jesus. But, to her surprise, Jesus sided with Mary. The conversation probably went something like this:

Martha: Excuse me, Jesus. Can I have a little word with you in the other room?

Jesus: Yes, Martha, of course. By the way, everything is so sparkling clean in your beautiful home. And something smells awfully delicious.

Martha: Well, that's what I wanted to talk to you about. I don't know if you noticed, but I've been very busy all afternoon trying to make the house nice and prepare a home-cooked meal for you.

Jesus: Yes, and I really appreciate that.

Martha: You see, the problem is, my sister hasn't gotten off her skinny butt from the moment you arrived.

Jesus: Oh, dear. Are you annoyed with her?

Martha: Just a skosh. You see, I wish *I* could just sit and spend time with you and listen to you talk like she does. It's like food for my soul. There's nothing that makes me happier.

Jesus: So why don't you?

Martha: Because I have a household to run, and you're my guest. And, more to the point, you're also Mary's guest, but she won't lift a finger to help.

Jesus: Well, just drop what you're doing and come sit with us.

Martha: But who's going to tend to the dinner? I mean, the chocolate-peanut-butter pie isn't going to make itself. What I'd *really* like is for you to tell Mary that she needs to march herself into the kitchen, put on an apron, and get to work.

Jesus: Martha, you're a dear friend, and have a kind and loving heart. But don't let your sense of responsibility for things of this world overtake what matters most: your spiritual well-being.

Martha: What do you mean?

Jesus: Well, sinning isn't limited to things like sexual immorality, greed, or jealousy. Sometimes, becoming overly invested in your job, or your children, or even your housekeeping duties can put a wedge between you and God. Like today. I would rather have had you with me all afternoon, even if that meant we would have only a crust of bread for dinner, than have you chained to the kitchen preparing a seven-course meal.

Martha: So you're saying *Mary* is doing the right thing?

Jesus: Well, what I am saying is, when you surrender your life to God and follow me, the burdens of this world will be lifted from your shoulders. But sometimes that means putting down the feather duster, taking the afternoon off, and spending some quality time with me and our Heavenly Father.

Martha: Forgive me, Lord. You're right. Sometimes I get so caught up in wanting to please everyone else, I lose sight of what's most important. Let me slip out of these oven mitts and pull up a seat by you and what's-her-face in the family room.

Jesus: Grace be with you, my child.

No question, being a hard worker is an admirable quality. But we can destroy ourselves and our relationships if we use the demands of our daily lives as an excuse to neglect God or the people close to us. Set aside some time every single day for the Lord and for the most important people in your life. That's the best way to fulfill God's purpose and lead a balanced and joyful life.

WHAT DO YOU THINK?

- Does Jesus' answer to Martha mean that God does not favor hard work? How do you balance having a strong work ethic to fulfill your worldly responsibilities with setting aside time for the Lord?
- Martha was missing valuable fellowship time with Jesus. Do you think there were other negative effects of her obsessing over her household duties and Mary's refusal to help?
- Have you ever lashed out or judged someone who you felt wasn't pulling their weight? How would Jesus have advised you to handle that situation?
- Sometimes putting down work and spending time with family, friends, or God means your job won't get done on time or won't be the highest quality. Has that ever happened to you? If so, how did you feel? Did you have any regrets?

Chapter 48

HEAVENLY GLORY: MY EXCLUSIVE SNEAK PREVIEW

(MATTHEW 16:13–28; 17:1–9; MARK 8:27–38; 9:2–10; LUKE 9:28–36)

Dear Diary,

So much has happened in the last few days, where do I start? I do have one piece of great news. But I also need to tell you about two bonehead things I did. Sometimes, I seriously wonder whether I should just go back to fishing and leave this spiritual stuff to the guys who have more upstairs, if you know what I mean.

First, the good news. I have reason to believe that I'm one of Jesus' favorites! In fact, I'm pretty sure I've clinched the number-one spot. We were all together the other night and Jesus asked, "Who do you think I am?" And I answered right away: "You are the Christ, the Son of the living God" (Matt. 16:16). I didn't think I was saying anything all that earth-shattering. It seems obvious to me, but apparently, this isn't so obvious to the rest of the world because Jesus told me that God himself had revealed that truth to me. That made me feel really good, like God must have some extra-special purpose for my life.

Then, Jesus told me something that completely blew me away. He said I would be given the keys to the Kingdom of Heaven! It sounds super exciting, although I don't really know what it means. I don't think he means I'm going to be locking and unlocking the doors to heaven, like some sort of security guard or custodian. Jesus said something about me having authority on earth to make decisions that are related to heaven. Not sure yet exactly what my job responsibilities will be, but I bet they're gonna be huge. But, I have to be honest: as happy as I am about all of this, it's also overwhelming. When he was talking to me about it, it was like my head was spinning. And then, just when things were going so well, I had to open my big mouth and blow it— BIG time.

I was still trying to figure out what it might mean to have the keys to the Kingdom of Heaven, so I was only half-listening when Jesus started telling all of us what was coming up. But then Jesus said something that caught my immediate attention. He said he would have to suffer at the hands of the Jewish religious leaders and that they would actually kill him. I was so shocked that I half yelled at him: "No, stop talking like that! They can't touch you!" Then, Jesus looked me right in the eye and said, "Get behind me, Satan! You are a stumbling block to me, for you are not setting your mind on the things of God, but on the things of men" (Matt. 16:23).

I thought, did I just hear him correctly? Did he just call me Satan? All I said was I didn't want him to die. Okay, maybe that wasn't the right thing to say. Fine. But Satan? The prince of darkness? The lord of all evil?! Jesus then said something about his fate being part of God's plan. And he implied that I was trying to tempt him to turn his back on God's will. That was definitely NOT my intention. I still didn't quite understand what made Jesus turn on me, but I sure felt like a jerk, just the same. But live and learn. I hope I won't make that kind of mistake again. So, that was idiot-move number one.

A few days later, Jesus told John, James, and me to follow him up the mountain. We had a nice talk on the way up. I was trying to do some damage control following my apparently evil suggestion that I didn't want him to die. So I just kept it light and chatty. When we got to the top of the mountain, all of a sudden, Jesus changed before our very eyes. His face became as bright as the sun, and his clothes were pure white. It was like he had been transformed into a different kind of creature. And then John and James and I could see Moses and the prophet Elijah standing there by Jesus. The three of them were chatting, just having a regular ol' conversation. We were all so shocked! John and James just stood there with their mouths open, but I felt like I needed to say something.

So, trying to be helpful, I offered to build three tents, one for Jesus, one for Moses, and one for Elijah. The minute those words left my mouth, I realized how stupid they were. Seriously, Peter? Build them tents? Like Jesus, Moses, and Elijah were going to spend the weekend on the mountain watching sunsets and sitting around the bonfire making s'mores? What is wrong with me? Jesus must have been thinking, 'Well, maybe I was a little hasty in selecting Peter for the job of minding the gates of heaven. Maybe I should appoint him to some less important job in the afterlife, like sizing new angels for their wings. Or repairing their harps when they have mid-air collisions while flying around in the clouds." Anyway, that was idiot-move number two.

The next thing I knew, this bright cloud kinda swallowed us up, and I heard a voice from heaven say: "This is my beloved Son, in whom I am well pleased. Listen to him" (Matt. 17:5). The guys and I were so scared that we immediately fell to the ground. It was like we were here on earth but somehow standing on the edge of heaven, looking in. It was all very cool, but also very terrifying.

But then Jesus walked over and touched each one of us and said, "Don't be afraid." We got up and Moses and Elijah were gone and Jesus looked just like he does every day. I'm so glad that James and John were with me and saw it all too, so I don't have to wonder if I imagined it all. We have talked about it a lot since that day, but we don't really know what to make of it.

It's weird. I've never been so happy in my life. I was selected for a great honor by our Lord and Savior, and he gave me a glimpse into the spiritual world. But I'm also very anxious. I keep wondering if I'm worthy of all this. I sure keep saying stupid things. What if I fail and let Jesus down? I keep reminding myself that he knew what he was getting when he picked me, warts and all. Or at least I think he knew all of that. I'll have to pray hard on this one.

In love and peace,
Peter

WHAT DO YOU THINK?

- Why do you think Peter was the Lord's first choice for holding the keys to heaven?

- Peter understandably felt bad when Jesus said: "Get behind me, Satan!" Do you think Jesus was trying to make Peter feel bad? If not, why did he use such harsh language?

- Jesus' transformation on top of the mountain is referred to as the Transfiguration. What was the purpose of the Transfiguration?

- Why do you think God wanted Moses and Elijah present during the Transfiguration? What did they represent in that moment?

- Why do you think Jesus did not bring all twelve apostles to witness the glory of the Transfiguration?

Chapter 49

YOUR FINANCIAL ADVISOR'S FAVORITE PARABLE

(MATTHEW 25:14–30)

Jesus liked to tell stories to help his disciples and other followers understand more about God and his kingdom. Today we call these stories "parables." One of Jesus' more famous parables starts with a wealthy master who decided to go on a long trip. Before he left, he needed to entrust his money to three of his servants.

The master gave the first servant five talents, the second servant two talents, and the third servant one talent. A talent was a kind of money, and each talent would be worth hundreds of thousands of dollars in today's currency. In other words, even one talent was a lot of dough. But the master made clear that he wasn't giving the servants this money for keeps. Instead, he was giving it to them so they could use it to make more money, for the master, while he was away on his trip.

When the master returned, he called in the servants to see how they had done. The first and second servants had doubled the master's money. The master thanked and praised them, telling each of them: "Well done, good and faithful servant. You have been faithful over a few things, I will set you over many things. Enter into the joy of your lord" (Matt. 25:21, 23).

Then the third guy showed up. He told his master, "I know you're mean and nasty, and I was scared of what you might do if I invested and lost your money. So I played it safe and buried it in the ground. But I dug it up and brushed off the dirt; so here it is. Take it all back. I didn't lose a single penny."

But the master was not at all happy with this guy and called him a "wicked and slothful servant" (Matt. 25:26). "How come you didn't at least put the money in a bank where it could have earned a few dollars of interest?" He was so upset that he ordered the talent to be taken away and given to the servant who had started out with five talents. Then he sent the third servant to "the outer darkness, where there will be weeping and gnashing of teeth" (Matt. 25:30). Jesus didn't share with us exactly what happens in the place of "outer darkness." However, people don't normally gnash their teeth when they're having a good time, so it's safe to assume it's not a place you want to be.

In this story, the master represents God, and the servants represent us. And the story demonstrates that God rewards people who make the most out of whatever gifts he bestows upon them. We all have gifts, and we will all choose how to use those gifts. The people who waste their gifts and opportunities by wallowing in fear, laziness, or lack of faith suffer the consequences both in this life and the next. The fact is, just like in a game of poker, in life we all start with a bunch of playing cards. Some of us are dealt four aces, and some of us are dealt a pair of deuces. But our ability to win the jackpot at the end of our lives and to feel good about what we accomplished and what we became often has little to do with the cards we start with. Instead, our accomplishments depend more on our attitude, our actions, and whether or not we decide to ask God into our hearts.

So don't bury your talents in a hole in the ground. Use them well and do not squander your short time here on earth.

WHAT DO YOU THINK?

- This parable seems to show that God doesn't want us playing it *too* safe with our lives here on earth. What are some ways we might be burying our gifts in the sand and missing out on God's rewards for us?
- What are some risks that we can take in our lives that God would favor? What types of risks should we avoid?
- Can you think of someone who had many advantages but squandered them all? Do you know anyone who started out with little but turned their lives into something great? Comparing the two, what lessons can you apply to your own life?

Chapter 50

WHEN LIFE IN THE FAST LANE ENDS UP IN A DITCH

(LUKE 15:11–32)

Another one of Jesus' parables focuses on a man and his two sons. The older son worked hard on his dad's farm and stayed out of trouble. This older son, we'll call him Goody-Two-Shoes, probably wasn't much fun at parties, but no doubt he could make a horse stall shine. The younger brother—we'll call him Lizard—was the wild child.

When his dad was still quite healthy and not even thinking about dying, the younger son came and asked for his share of his inheritance. In other words, Lizard wanted, right at that very minute, the portion of his dad's money he should only receive after his father died. Needless to say, Lizard wasn't going to win any awards for son of the year. But his dad agreed, and Lizard left the farm as quickly as he could, off to see the world with a heck of a lot of cash jingling around in his pockets.

For a little while, Lizard seemed to be living the good life. He partied until all hours of the night, bought lots of really cool stuff, and rubbed elbows with the beautiful people. But, before long, his pockets were empty, and the beautiful people no longer had any use for him. Feeling as empty as his pockets, Lizard had to go feed pigs just to make enough money to eat. Even then, he went hungry most of the time, and no one ever offered him any help.

One day when he was watching the pigs fill their stomachs while listening to his own stomach growl, it dawned on him that even his father's servants had it better. So he decided to go crawling back to his dad. By this point, Lizard realized that giving himself over to sin had not made him happy at all. In fact, it ultimately made him miserable. And he now felt truly sorry for hurting his father, the person who loved him more than anyone else in the world.

On his long walk home, Lizard rehearsed the speech he would give his father, hoping his dad would let him hang around as a servant. But long before Lizard reached the gate of the family farm, his dad saw him coming and ran to meet him, grabbing him and clinging tightly to him and kissing him. Lizard tried to deliver his spiel: "Father, I have sinned against heaven and in your sight. I am no longer worthy to be called your son" (Luke 15:21). But the father loved his son so much and had such compassion for him that he instantly rejected his son's proposal to be just one of his dad's hired hands. Instead, the father forgave him and rejoiced that Lizard was back home. Then he called for his servants to whip up a fancy party, complete with the family's prized fatted calf, so everyone could celebrate.

Clearly, this parable reminds us that, no matter how much we mess up, God is ready to welcome us home when we truly are sorry and ask his forgiveness. Everyone sins, even though we know that giving in to temptation is a recipe for disaster. But if we keep Jesus in our hearts, we will eventually make our way back to our Lord and his infinite love for us.

But the tale of Goody-Two-Shoes and Lizard, which most people call the story of the Prodigal Son, didn't end with everyone celebrating Lizard's homecoming. Because when Goody-Two-Shoes heard about Lizard's party, he got mad and complained to his dad. I imagine the conversation went something like: "How could you?! My loser brother told you he couldn't even wait for you to bite the dust before getting his greedy little Lizard hands on your money. Then he takes that cash and goes on an extended party binge, leaving Yours Truly to plow the fields, milk the cows, and clean the stinkin' horse stalls. Did it ever occur to you that maybe I want a big party, with belly dancers and snake charmers? Just think of all I've done for you through the years. How come you never brought in a nine-piece band from Jerusalem for me? And, while we're on the subject, why did HE get the fatted calf?!"

I bet you're totally sympathetic with Goody-Two-Shoes right now. Sometimes it seems like being the nice guy leaves you doing all the work while the cheaters, liars, and jerks get all of the recognition, the awesome toys, and the coolest friends. It can make us wonder why we even try! But scratch beneath the surface, and you'll see that people who live sinful lives away from God are unhappy, empty, and missing meaning or purpose in their lives. The promise of glitz, excitement, and joy that supposedly comes with living the high life ultimately turns out to be a big fat lie.

As you might have suspected, the father in the story of the Prodigal Son represents our Heavenly Father, and the sons represent us. Whether you relate more to Lizard or Goody-Two-Shoes probably depends on where you are in your life's journey. Maybe you have tried to cut God out of your life and are afraid you can never return. This story should give you great hope because it shows that God is always ready to forgive and to restore you to a place of honor.

Or maybe you've spent your life trying to live the right way and are frustrated because it doesn't seem to be working out so well for you. Then you need to hear the father's words to his older son: "You are always with me, and all that is mine is yours" (Luke 15:31). In other words, if we live our lives according to our Lord's will, we will receive our inheritance as children of God: true joy, peace, and eternal life.

And when we have messed up and wandered away, we can rejoice in knowing that God will always welcome us back. Just as he did with the younger son, God will be ready to "celebrate and be glad, for this, your brother, was dead, and is alive again. He was lost, and is found" (Luke 15:32).

Amen!

WHAT DO YOU THINK?

- It often seems like some people who indulge in a life of sin enjoy themselves. Do you think they really do?
- In our story, when Lizard hit rock bottom, he went back to his father and asked for forgiveness. Have you ever gotten so caught up in sin that you were afraid God wouldn't forgive you? How did you handle that?
- Have you ever felt like the older brother in our story? Do you feel like you're trying hard to do the right thing and obey God while sinners get all the rewards and have all the fun? Did that feeling lead you to sin? How did that work out for you?
- In deciding on how to focus your time and efforts, how do you balance long-lasting rewards versus short-term pleasures?

DID I HEAR THAT RIGHT?
DID JESUS JUST
COMPARE HER TO
A COCKER SPANIEL?

(MATTHEW 5:1–12; 15:21–28; MARK 7:24–30)

Dear Diary,

I have to be honest. Sometimes I miss the simple life I left behind. Don't get me wrong, I'm not saying I regret my decision to follow Jesus. He is the best thing that ever happened to me. But life on the road can be tough. I miss my house in my quiet little fishing village of Capernaum. And I really miss sleeping in my own bed. Sometimes I wish I could have just one day back from my old life, getting up early in the morning and taking the boat out. Then, at the end of the day, coming home to a nice quiet dinner.

But usually when I'm getting most nostalgic, something happens to remind me that this life with Jesus is so worth all my sacrifices. That's what happened today, here in Tyre and Sidon, where there are a lot of non-Jews, the so-called "gentiles." We had gone with Jesus into the home of one of the Jewish people to try to get away from the crowds. Out of the blue, this gentile woman came in and threw herself down on the ground, right at Jesus' feet. She begged him to help her young daughter who was possessed by demons. I felt so sorry for her. You could see that she was in agony, worrying about her kid.

But Jesus told her that, because she wasn't Jewish, he couldn't use his miraculous powers to help her. He explained he had been sent for "the lost sheep of the house of Israel" and could not "take the children's bread and throw it to the dogs" (Matt. 15:24, 26).

I thought, "Wow. That's pretty harsh, even if she is a gentile." But the woman didn't even flinch. She just told Jesus that "even the dogs eat the crumbs which fall from their masters' table" (Matt. 15:27). Jesus turned and looked at her then, and he was smiling now. "You've got a lot of faith," he told her. "I'm really impressed. Your daughter is healed. Go home to her now."

After watching this whole scene unfold before my eyes, I think I'm finally understanding, on a deeper level, what Jesus has been teaching us. It goes back to what he preached during the sermon that he gave on the mountain in Galilee, right after I started following him. He said God values qualities like humility, kindness, and love, not pride, ambition, self-promotion, and competition with others. Back then, Jesus said the "gentle" people will "inherit the earth" (Matt. 5:1-12). He said it's not the rich and powerful who will receive life's ultimate rewards but the "poor in spirit" (Matt. 5:3). He also said the peacemakers and the ones who show mercy are favored by God and will receive his mercy (Matt. 5:7-9).

I don't think I really believed all this when I first heard it. Maybe it's because my dad was a bit of a tough guy, a fisherman who made his living in the harsh conditions on the open sea. I always wanted to be like my dad: self-reliant and strong. Dad taught me to never let anyone get the best of me. So the idea that God rewards those who are meek, humble, and compassionate just didn't fit with what I was taught when I was growing up.

But my eyes were opened when I saw a mother who loved her child so much that she would grovel at the feet of a man she had never met and not even get insulted when he compared her to a common dog. She was willing to do all that just to save her little girl. In her selfless humility, in her willingness to swallow every ounce of pride for the sake of love, I saw a strength and power like I had never seen before. Light poured from her as she looked up at Jesus while kneeling on the ground, and her face shone like the sun when Jesus praised her faith. In that moment I finally understood fully Jesus' message that grace, humility, selflessness, and love ultimately will triumph over selfish pride, a rebellious spirit, or a stubborn refusal to seek God.

I've just been lying here tonight wondering what else might be waiting for me on this incredible journey. What other glorious truths will God reveal to me?

In love and peace,
Peter

WHAT DO YOU THINK?

- This story shows us that the ultimate expression of strength can arise from humility, self-sacrifice, and love. Where does that strength come from? Are some people just born with it?
- Do you believe the flipside of the above statement is true? Are aggressiveness, self-promotion, and arrogance actually signs of weakness? Describe some examples of this behavior from our world today.
- Have you ever had to swallow your pride and humble yourself in the interest of a greater good? Or have you witnessed someone else who has done so? Describe what happened.

Chapter 52

COULDN'T YOU WAIT UNTIL MY BODY WAS COLD BEFORE YOU SOLD ALL MY STUFF?

(JOHN 11:1–53)

One of Jesus' closest friends was Lazarus, the brother of Martha, the workaholic homemaker we read about earlier, and her less diligent but spiritually faithful sister, Mary. Just before Passover, Lazarus got deathly ill, and Martha and Mary sent for Jesus. As Jesus' besties, the sisters knew all about his miracles and wanted him to use some of his healing powers to save their dying brother. Surprisingly, Jesus didn't seem to be in any hurry to swoop in and cure poor Lazarus. Even after he heard about his friend's illness, Jesus stayed where he was for another couple of days.

By the time Jesus arrived at Martha and Mary's house in the village of Bethany, Lazarus had already been dead for four days. Apparently, it wasn't beneath Martha and Mary to try to send Jesus on a major guilt trip. They said something like: "Gee, Lord, if you didn't take your sweet ol' time getting here, you might have been able to save our brother, and he wouldn't be wrapped like a mummy and rotting in a cave right now." Of course, they said it in a much nicer way, but that was the gist of it.

Jesus watched everyone mourning the death of Lazarus, and then he did something that may seem unexpected for the Son of God: he "wept" (John 11:35). Yes, our Lord and Savior, who had the power to work miracles and a direct pipeline to our Heavenly Father, shed real-life tears over the passing of his buddy. I found this was an important piece of information when I first learned about Jesus' tearful reaction. It made me like Jesus even more because it reminded me he was truly human and shared the pain we all feel when we lose someone we really care about.

When I was a kid, I would sometimes lie in bed at night worrying about the day my mom and dad would pass away. The thought of losing them forever made me so sad, even though I always believed in heaven. But the idea of a perfect, happy life after death gave me little comfort in those moments because I figured it would still be years—probably decades—before I would see my parents again after their passing.

And let's face it, we don't really know what heaven is or what happens there. Do we truly get to see the people we have loved in this life when we get there? If so, will they look the same or will they be some radiant, whitewashed, angelic version of their earthly selves? Will we even recognize them? And what about our pets? Would heaven really be heaven if, when I get there (and I'm hoping that I do!), I find out that Dukey, Felix, Calvin, Larry, and Arnold didn't make the cut? And even if everyone I loved is there, do we get more than just a quick hello at the "welcome to heaven" party? Does everyone then go back to flying around the clouds playing their harps or, in the case of Larry and Arnold, swimming around the clouds? (Yes, Larry and Arnold were my pet fish.) The more I thought about heaven and all of its mysteries, the less it did to relieve my sadness over someday losing my parents.

But I was reassured when I learned that Jesus cried at the death of Lazarus. That short verse convinced me that God "gets it." Through Jesus, God experienced firsthand the heartache of losing someone he truly loved. The Lord therefore has to understand that, at least for me, heaven won't feel like an entirely happy ending if, when I get there, I don't get to be with the people I loved here on earth. And, because we don't know much about what heaven will be like, it can't completely ease our sadness at losing someone we love. All that, just from a few tears shed by Jesus? Absolutely.

After Jesus collected himself, he went to Lazarus' tomb, which was a cave sealed with a large rock. He asked that the stone be moved aside so he could get inside. Martha, true to her reputation as a clean-freak, told Jesus this might not be the best idea because her brother's body would surely stink by now. Jesus disregarded his well-meaning but uptight friend and had some big, burly guys move the stone. Then he stepped back and started to pray.

> Jesus lifted up his eyes, and said, "Father, I thank you that you listened to me. I know that you always listen to me, but because of the multitude standing around I said this, that they may believe that you sent me." When he had said this, he cried with a loud voice, "Lazarus, come out!" (John 11:41–43)

And Lazarus did come out! He was draped in the cloth that they had wrapped his body in, but it probably didn't take long for Mary, Martha, and their friends to unwrap him. Everyone rejoiced at the incredible miracle that had taken place. No doubt, they celebrated over a wonderful meal prepared by none other than Martha, with hopefully at least a little help from Mary.

But there was one group who wasn't at all happy about Lazarus rejoining the living. You guessed it: the Pharisees. They did not find this miracle a reason to believe in Jesus. In fact, it just made them hate him more.

It was bad enough that Jesus was healing people. But bringing people back from the dead? This took it to a whole new level. In the Pharisees' words: "If we leave [Jesus] alone like this, everyone will believe in him, and the Romans will come and take away both our place and our nation" (John 11:48). The miracle of Lazarus coming back from the dead was the final straw for Jewish leaders. They began working in earnest to devise a plan to have him killed.

WHAT DO YOU THINK?

- Why do you think Jesus didn't rush right to Bethany when he heard that Lazarus was dying?
- If Jesus knew that he had the power to bring Lazarus back from the dead, why was he so sad that he cried?
- Describe what you think heaven is like. Do you worry that it won't be perfect? Or do you have lingering doubts that it won't live up to its reputation? Can you overcome those concerns by relying on your trust in God?
- Some people claim to have died and entered heaven and then returned to life. Do you believe they truly entered heaven? Do you believe what they say about their experience? Do you think God would permit that? Could there be other explanations for their experience?

Chapter 53

THE TRUE FACE OF STRENGTH AND POWER

(MATTHEW 21:10–13; 22:15–22; MARK 11:15–18; 12:13–17;
LUKE 19:41–48; 20:19–26; JOHN 2:13–17)

Jesus was an interesting guy. He grew up in a family without a lot of money and worked as a carpenter until about the age of thirty. He then started his ministry, which lasted only about three years before he was executed by the world's most powerful government. And yet, despite Jesus' humble beginnings and incredibly short ministry, he had an influence over the world like no other single human being who has ever walked the face of the earth.

He turned on its head religious beliefs that prevailed for thousands of years: that we can earn God's favor by complying with a bunch of religious rules and performing ceremonial rituals and sacrifices. Jesus taught that the true way to eternal life is through humility, forgiveness, loving one another, and surrendering ourselves to God. It is difficult to imagine how this one man, who was born in a barn and worked as a common laborer for most of his adult life, could set in motion a religion that more than 2,000 years later has well over two billion followers, more than any other religion in the world. It's an understatement to say there was something very special about this person.

But what was Jesus, the man, really like? The Bible gives us only glimpses into some aspects of his personality and character. Quite clearly, he was a loving and gentle soul who was not easily provoked to anger. We also know that he was without sin. But what about the other parts of his personality? Did Jesus have a good sense of humor? Was he athletic? Was he a morning person or a night owl? Did he like to cook? Was he fun at parties? We just don't know. We do know that Jesus was a rule follower for the most part, but he could also be a bit edgy at times, like when he healed people on the Sabbath or argued with the Pharisees.

Jesus did that a lot because the Pharisees were always looking for ways to trip him up and make him look bad. One day, they came to him with a question about whether the Jewish people should pay their taxes. At that time, the top dog of the Roman Empire was Tiberius Caesar, who ruled over the Jewish people with an iron fist. Understandably, the Jews despised him and resented having to pay taxes to him. In asking their question, the Pharisees knew that if Jesus said "Don't pay your taxes," they could rat him out to the Roman authorities, who probably would throw Jesus in jail—or worse. Removing him from the equation in this way would solve the Pharisees' dilemma of Jesus' rising influence over the Jewish people and his threat to their power and authority.

But if Jesus said "Yes, just pay the darn taxes," then the Jewish people would think: "Uh-oh, looks like Jesus just joined

Team Caesar. Today he's telling us to pay the taxes, but what next? We'll probably see him sitting in the front row of Caesar's next gladiator versus ferocious-lion grudge match. And he'll probably be rooting for the lion." But, of course, Jesus gave an answer that was even craftier than the question, and he wasn't fooled about why they were asking it.

"Why do you test me, you hypocrites? Show me the tax money" (Matt. 22:18–19). So the Pharisees brought him a coin, and Jesus asked, "Whose picture is on this coin?" "It's Caesar, of course," the Pharisees answered. Then Jesus said, "Give therefore to Caesar the things that are Caesar's, and to God the things that are God's" (Matt. 22:21). Even the Pharisees were impressed by that answer, and they couldn't think of anything else to say.

In essence, Jesus was telling the Pharisees (and us) that humans live in a world with laws put in place by those in charge. As long as we're still residents of planet earth, we need to play by the rules, which unfortunately includes paying our taxes. In other words, God didn't send Jesus to start a political revolution, so Jesus wasn't encouraging the people to give Caesar a poke in the eye. On the contrary, Jesus taught us to respect earthly authority even while reminding us that God is our ultimate authority.

Then there was the time Jesus went to pray in the temple in Jerusalem. When he arrived, he was appalled to see that this exalted worldwide center of the Jewish faith had been turned into the ancient world's equivalent of a shopping mall. The temple was overrun by greedy money-changers and peddlers of doves, livestock, and all kinds of other merchandise. They set up shop in the temple, not so they could worship God, but to wheel and deal. Jesus went ballistic when he saw that his Father's most holy place of worship had been turned into a "den of robbers" (Mark 11:15–17).

Jesus started overturning the tables and benches where these men were conducting their business. He chased them away and then banned any such activity inside the temple from that point on. Jesus must have displayed raw physical power to overtake this entire group of men. No doubt, they wouldn't have given up their prime locations in the temple if they were not truly frightened of Jesus.

So what do these two stories tell us about Jesus' personality? Certainly, when Jesus overpowered the greedy merchants in the temple, his strength took on a physical dimension. But, arguably, his strength was no less apparent when he answered the Pharisees' tax question. Instead of physical strength, the tax response displayed strength of character and conviction.

Jesus proved that true strength and courage are not what you see from the loudmouths, the bullies, the lawbreakers, or the bad guys of the world. Jesus had unsurpassed compassion, self-control, and love, and yet he also displayed a fiery intensity, fortitude, and unlimited power to stand up for what is right. This combination of qualities made him uniquely qualified to transform the world forever and light our path to God's kingdom and eternal salvation.

WHAT DO YOU THINK?

- Many of us have a fairly two-dimensional picture in our heads of Jesus, especially if we don't communicate with him regularly in prayer. Do you feel like you have a true connection to Jesus? Do you have a vision of Jesus' human qualities?

- As Christians, should we obey people in authority in every situation? If not, describe a situation where God would approve of you disobeying or rebelling against those in authority.

- In addition to government officials, what are other examples of authority figures? Do they deserve the same level of deference as our government? How should we act if we believe someone in authority, such as a teacher in school, is acting improperly?

- Jesus managed to keep his cool even when many people around him demonstrated deplorable conduct. Why did the situation in the Temple cause him to react with such outrage?

Chapter 54

AM I GOING CRAZY? OR IS THAT OUR TAX COLLECTOR PERCHED UP IN THAT TREE?

(LUKE 19:1–10)

Jesus was generating more and more buzz as he traveled around Judea. People were hearing about this guy from Galilee who was healing the sick, calming the seas, feeding thousands, and preaching about God's love and mercy. They would line the streets as he passed through their towns, just trying to get a glimpse of him. That is what happened one day when Jesus and his apostles made their way through the city of Jericho.

Now there was a man in town who desperately wanted to lay eyes on Jesus. His name was Zacchaeus, and he was the chief tax collector in this region. Like Zacchaeus, many tax collectors were Jewish, but were working for the Roman Empire. And that alone made them pretty unpopular. To make matters worse, they typically took more money than the Romans required and kept that money for themselves. Basically, these guys were traitors to their own people and also cheats, so the Jewish people couldn't stand them.

Zacchaeus was also short. By the time he heard that Jesus was coming to town, the streets were already packed. Even standing on his tippy toes, Zacchaeus was never going to get a glimpse of Jesus, and no one was going to let that little creep squeeze past them for a better view. So Zacchaeus climbed a sycamore tree along the road, giving him the height he needed to see it all.

When Jesus approached, he stopped next to the tree, looked up, and saw Zacchaeus peeking through the branches. Their interaction went something like this.

Jesus: Zacchaeus, is that you up there?

Zacchaeus: Nobody up here but us birds. Tweet, tweet!

Jesus: Zacchaeus, I can see you! What are you doing up there?

Zacchaeus: Oh, don't mind me. I'm just looking for a ripe pomegranate.

Jesus: That's a sycamore. There are no pomegranates up there.

Zacchaeus: Oh, did I say pomegranate? I meant to say fig.

Jesus: Were you trying to sneak a peek at me?

Zacchaeus: Maybe.

Jesus: Well, get down from there!

Zacchaeus: No. I don't want to.

Jesus: Look, I'd like you to come down and take me to your house for dinner. I'd like to spend some time with you.

Zacchaeus: With me? Do you know who I am?

Jesus: Yes, I know all about you.

Zacchaeus: Then you know that I'm not a good person. Don't you hear all these people booing and hissing right now? I've cheated a lot of people and done a lot of bad things in my life. So, please just leave me alone; go away and pretend that you never saw me.

Jesus: Zacchaeus, you are right about one thing: you have done a lot of bad things to a lot of people. But you're not a bad person. There is still hope for you. That's why I want to come to your house and have dinner with you. I want you and everyone else to know I have come to heal the damaged and brokenhearted people who need God's love the most, and you are among them. Now please, come down.

Zacchaeus: I can't.

Jesus: What's wrong now?

Zacchaeus: My sandal is wedged between these branches. I'm stuck!

After Jesus helped Zacchaeus get out of the tree, they went to his house and shared a nice meal. Zacchaeus was so grateful for the love and forgiveness Jesus showed to him that he promised to give half of everything he owned to the poor. He also vowed to pay back every person he had ever cheated, saying he would give them four times the amount that he had taken. During his ministry, Jesus showed that he had the power to heal physical illnesses and to resurrect those who had died a physical death. And his interaction with Zacchaeus proved that Jesus also had the power to give renewed life to those who had died a spiritual death.

We don't know why Zacchaeus had been so motivated by wealth and power that he was willing to lie and cheat his own people. Maybe he was trying to compensate for some feelings of insecurity; perhaps he had been bullied all his life because he was so short. But Jesus showed Zacchaeus that he could live an honorable life according to God's plan and treat people fairly and with kindness. That way, Zacchaeus could earn the love and respect he so longed for.

We all have our insecurities. But God's love can renew and revive us today, giving us the power to act honorably and with mercy, just like it did for Zacchaeus.

WHAT DO YOU THINK?

- Jesus' interactions with Zacchaeus highlight second chances and redemption. Why did Zacchaeus need a personal encounter with Jesus to change his heart and turn his life around?
- As the local tax collector, Zacchaeus' sins were very visible and public. Does that make his sins more deserving of punishment than people's private sins?
- What are other examples of "public" sins? What are examples of "private" sins? In what ways can private sins be more destructive than public ones?
- Do you think people often pursue money and power because they desperately desire the respect and admiration of others? What are other ways some people try to earn respect and admiration?
- Is being respected important to you? If so, how do you try to earn it?

Chapter 55

THE WORST NIGHT OF MY LIFE

(MATTHEW 26:17–75; MARK 14:12–72; LUKE 22:7–62; JOHN 13; 18:1–27)

Dear Diary,

How can I even describe the past twenty-four hours? It's been horrible. It's like living in my worst nightmare, but I just can't wake up. Jesus is gone. They arrested him in the middle of the night. The Pharisees—cowards that they are—knew better than to try to come get him during the day when all the people could see what they were doing.

I think they are going to try to have him executed. Can they do that? Can they kill someone for being too merciful? For being too wise? For telling people to love God and each other? I want to believe it can't happen, but I know better. The Romans can kill anybody for anything at any moment.

And that's not even the worst of it. As horrible as I feel about what's happening to Jesus, I feel even worse about myself. I sank to a new low last night. I did something I vowed I would NEVER do. I pretended I was not a follower of Jesus. In fact, I swore I had never even met him. And I didn't deny my ties to Jesus just once, but three separate times in just a few hours.

I wish I could say I don't know why I did that, but I do know. I was scared. I always thought of myself as a pretty tough guy. I spent a lot of years fishing on the open seas, and you can't do that if you scare easily. And I've never backed down if someone was messing with me or my family. But tonight, I proved that deep down, I'm just a coward. And none of what happened is making any sense to me. Anyway, let me back up a bit and tell you the whole sad story.

The week actually started out pretty good, with us arriving in Jerusalem to celebrate the Passover. And, I gotta say, our entry into the city was unbelievable. Jesus was riding on this young donkey, and the people ran out to meet us, like Jesus was some sort of international celebrity. They cut off palm branches and waved them at us and placed them on the road in front of us and yelled things like: "Hosanna to the son of David! Blessed is he who comes in the name of the Lord! Hosanna in the highest" (Matt. 21:9). It was pretty exciting.

Jesus spent a lot of the next few days preaching and teaching in the temple, and the crowds loved him because his words were like a breath of fresh air. But Jesus was also getting more and more critical of the Pharisees and other Jewish leaders, and it was obvious they were not happy. The other apostles and I knew things were getting a little risky, but we were certain Jesus would make everything right.

However, we really started to worry about how things would turn out last night while we were having our Passover dinner. Jesus seemed very solemn. At one point, he broke a loaf of bread into pieces and passed it to us along with a cup of wine. He told us the bread was his body and the wine was his blood and he was sharing it with us for the forgiveness of our sins. I was thinking: "Body and blood? What is he talking about?"

Jesus tried to explain, but it was so hard to follow. He said he knew the Jewish people were expecting God to send someone to rescue them from the Romans. But then he said, "That's not me." He told us that he came to earth to free us from the bondage of sin, and that he was the way to salvation. He then told us that, in order for him to fulfill God's purpose for his life here on earth, he would soon have to leave us. That's when a horrible feeling came over me.

What Jesus said next was even more disturbing. He predicted: "One of you is going to betray me tonight and the rest of you are going to let me down." I wasn't sure what that meant, but I was certain he was wrong about me—I would NEVER let Jesus down. "I don't care what anyone else does," I said loudly, "I will never turn my back on you. I'm ready to die with you." He then looked me square in the eye and said, "Most certainly I tell you that tonight, before the rooster crows, you will deny me three times" (Matt. 26:34). And, as it turns out, he was right. It's hard to put into words how much it hurts when I replay his words inside my head.

After that strange Passover dinner, Jesus wanted to go to the Garden of Gethsemane to pray. Jesus seemed very upset, and none of the rest of us knew what to say, so it was pretty quiet. Jesus told John, James, and me to sit and wait for him while he went deeper into the garden to pray alone. I was really trying to pray, but I was so completely drained from the week and that weird dinner conversation that I just couldn't keep my eyes open. Neither could James or John. Jesus kept coming back and waking us up and begging us to stay alert and pray, but none of us could hold out for more than a few minutes. It made me feel so weak and useless.

Eventually, Jesus came and poked us and said, "Get up. It's time." I looked up and saw a crowd of men coming with torches, clubs, and swords. As they got closer, we realized it was the Jewish religious leaders and their soldiers. Clearly, they were there on official business and were prepared for a fight. Then Judas stepped out from among them, walked up to Jesus, and kissed him on the cheek. Well, now we knew which one of us was going to betray Jesus!

Everyone was looking at Jesus, so I knew it was my opportunity to act. I grabbed the sword I had hidden under my cloak and started running toward the leader of that gang—I didn't even realize at the moment that it was Caiaphas, the Jewish high priest. As I swung my sword, Caiaphas' servant jumped in the way, and I felt my weapon sink into his flesh as I cut off his ear. Before I knew it, Jesus had stepped in. "Put your sword away, Peter. That's not how this is going to go. I must do what God has called me to do." Then Jesus reached out and touched the servant, and his ear was suddenly restored.

Instead of falling down and worshiping Jesus for this act of healing, the Jewish leaders and the guards took this as a sign to rough him up a little. They grabbed him and tied him up and started marching him away. And suddenly, all the courage and conviction drained out of me. I knew I could do some damage with my sword—I had proved it. But what was I supposed to do if Jesus didn't want me to fight? I decided to follow these thugs, but I hung back at a safe distance. I was scared, not just for Jesus, but also for myself. What if they decided to come get me for attacking the servant of the high priest?

They led Jesus through the city to the high priest's house. A bunch of people were huddled around a fire in the courtyard, so I went over to warm up. I noticed this young woman staring at me, so I tried to avoid looking at her. But she walked right up to me and said, "Aren't you a friend of that Jesus? I saw you with him earlier." I told her she was mistaken, that I didn't know him and had never even spoken to him. As the words left my lips, I felt so ashamed. But I was so scared they would take me away too.

She walked off, so I thought I was safe. But then a man started yelling that he had seen me with Jesus. "No way," I said. "I don't even know him!" The guy backed off and things got quiet again. Then, about an hour later, a third guy started in on me. "You're one of those Jesus guys," he said. "I know because I can tell that you're from Galilee."

I got really loud this time. "Man, I don't know what you are talking about!" (Luke 22:60). And right then, right at that second, I heard a rooster crow, and I remembered what Jesus said at dinner. He had been right. He had known exactly what I would do when I felt threatened. Right then, in the courtyard, I could see Jesus' face so clearly in my head that it was like he was standing right in front of me staring into my soul. I stumbled away from the fire, hid behind a tree, and sobbed.

I snuck away from the courtyard a little later. I'm still not sure what will happen to Jesus, but I wasn't going to be much help anyway. But now that I'm alone with my thoughts, I'm in total agony. I've been thinking about Judas—I can't believe he betrayed Jesus to the Jewish leaders. I heard a rumor that he got some silver for helping the leaders find Jesus in an isolated place. But am I really any better? I didn't get any silver, but I definitely denied Jesus, just to save my own life. And only a few hours after I vowed that I was ready to die with him.

Jesus knew me better than I knew myself. He knew for sure that I would deny him. He even knew exactly how many times I would do it. Does that mean my actions were already planned for me? I would love to believe that. It might lift some of this searing guilt away from my heart. But I just can't pretend that I didn't know what I was doing. I knew exactly what I was doing and saying. Nobody forced me to disown Jesus the way I did.

I feel like such a coward—and I'm still scared. What happens to me and the rest of the apostles if Jesus is executed or thrown in prison? Where will we go? What will we do? And how can I ever forget what I did to Jesus, my teacher and dear friend? I turned my back on him in his darkest hour. It's breaking my heart. I just wish he were here with me now, so I could tell him in person how sorry I am.

In bitterness and grief,
Peter

WHAT DO YOU THINK?

- The reception given to Jesus when he entered Jerusalem, which many Christian churches celebrate on Palm Sunday, represents the height of his approval and renown during his ministry here on earth. Why did he enter the city riding on a donkey, which was considered to be a lowly and common animal? Why would he choose a donkey instead of a more regal and spirited animal like a horse?

- What was the significance of the Last Supper, when Jesus told his disciples to eat the bread, which symbolized his body, and drink the wine, which symbolized his blood?

- Since Jesus knew ahead of time that Peter would deny him three times, does that mean Peter had no choice or free will to do otherwise? Assuming God can see the future, what does that mean for us? Is our fate sealed? Or do we have the ability to determine our own future?

Chapter 56

THE CRUCIFIXION: THE STORY AIN'T OVER YET

(MATTHEW 27:1–56; MARK 15:1–41; LUKE 22:63–71; 23:1–49;
JOHN 18:28–40; 19:1–37)

If you have ever doubted that evil exists, just take a look at the final days of Jesus' life. Jesus was the only person who ever lived on this earth who never sinned. His whole life was devoted to kindness, mercy, and love. And yet he was betrayed, beaten, spit on, taunted, and ultimately sent to death by the religious leaders of his own people. Why? Because he was gaining too many followers who also were devoting their lives to kindness, mercy, and love.

After Jesus was arrested in the Garden of Gethsemane, the Jewish temple police dragged him through the streets of Jerusalem to stand trial in the home of the high priest, Caiaphas. In the middle of the night, Jesus went on trial for his supposed crimes before the Sanhedrin, the governing council of Jewish priests, Pharisees, scribes, and elders. Our Lord stood alone before these men as they accused, interrogated, and derided him. They had witnesses show up to tell lies about Jesus, looking for some reason to put him to death. The men sitting in judgment of Jesus were the very same guys who had been plotting to kill him all along. For most of the time, Jesus said nothing at all.

But eventually Caiaphas directly asked Jesus: "Are you the Christ, the Son of the Blessed?" And Jesus answered this question. He said, "I am. You will see the Son of Man sitting at the right hand of Power, and coming with the clouds of the sky" (Mark 14:61–62). That was enough evidence for Caiaphas.

"This man just claimed to be the son of God," he said. "Any man who claims to be equal to God is committing blasphemy. We don't need any more witnesses. We all heard him!" The other leaders agreed, and they declared that he should be put to death for saying he was the son of God. Then they became even nastier. "Some began to spit on him, and to cover his face, and to beat him with fists, and to tell him, 'Prophesy!' The officers struck him with the palms of their hands" (Mark 14:65).

After the Jewish leaders got tired of torturing Jesus, they dragged him to Pontius Pilate, the Roman governor of the region. Although the Jews could sentence Jesus to death, they could not actually execute him; only the Romans could handle executions. So they needed Pilate to affirm the conviction and order that the deed be done. Pilate questioned Jesus for a while, but he found no evidence that Jesus had committed a crime worthy of death.

Pilate didn't really want to execute Jesus, so he offered to release him as a sort of Passover gift, as he always freed one Jewish prisoner every year at this time. So he said, "I'm going to release one prisoner today. It can be Jesus or Barabbas." Now Barabbas was a notorious criminal who had been found guilty of murder and a bunch of other horrible crimes. Clearly, Pilate expected the Jewish people to prefer Jesus to be walking around free rather than Barabbas. But Pilate underestimated how badly the Jewish leaders wanted Jesus dead. In fact, they rounded up a bunch of angry people to stand outside Pilate's house and shout for Barabbas to be released and for Jesus to be killed.

Pilate tried to reason with the crowd, but they just yelled louder: "Crucify! Crucify him!" (Luke 23:21). The crowd was getting so loud and so unruly that Pilate was afraid they were going to start rioting, so he finally gave in. Showing what a coward he was, Pilate then "took water and washed his hands before the multitude, saying, 'I am innocent of the blood of this righteous person. You see to it'" (Matt. 27:24). Essentially, Pilate was saying that he knew Jesus was innocent and was refusing to take the blame for sentencing him to death.

With that, Pilate released Barabbas and turned Jesus over to the Roman soldiers for execution. The soldiers beat Jesus and spit on him. They made him wear a purple robe and impaled his head with a crown of thorns, mocking him as the "King of the Jews." They then nailed him to a cross and planted the cross on top of Mount Golgotha, where he would die a slow, public death in front of his enemies as well as some of his followers and loved ones, including his own mother.

While Jesus hung on the cross, he said the incredible words, "Father, forgive them, for they don't know what they are doing" (Luke 23:34). In the depths of his suffering, Jesus' expression of forgiveness for the very people who were committing such horrible acts against him removed any doubt about why God sent Jesus to earth. He did not come to incite a political uprising to end the oppression of the Jewish people by the Roman Empire or to reform the Jewish religious leaders. Instead, he came to start a spiritual revolution that would change the world forever. With his final act of mercy while he was dying on the cross, Jesus showed us that the way to eternal life, joy, and fulfillment is not through earthly power, physical strength, or political might. It is through humility, kindness, and love for one another, even for our enemies.

In Jesus' final hours, the sun was darkened, and the temple veil was torn in two. And "Jesus, crying with a loud voice, said, 'Father, into your hands I commit my spirit!'" (Luke 23:46). Then Jesus breathed his last breath.

WHAT DO YOU THINK?

- Why do you think the Jewish leaders apprehended Jesus and put him on trial at night?
- Why didn't Jesus try to defend himself, either before the Sanhedrin or before Pontius Pilate?
- In Jesus' hour of need, where were the thousands of people who lined the streets and flocked to him during his ministry? What did the Jewish leaders do to deter the people from helping Jesus?

Chapter 57

A LARGE STONE WAS MOVED AND A GLORIOUS GATE WAS OPENED

(MATTHEW 27:57–66; 28:1–10; MARK 15:42–47; 16:1–13; LUKE 23:47–56; 24:1–35; JOHN 19:38–42; 20:1–18)

Even the Romans standing at the cross realized that a good man had just died. A follower of Jesus named Joseph, who was from the city of Arimathea, asked Pilate for Jesus' body. He wrapped it in linen and put the body in the tomb he had reserved for himself. Jesus' followers, numb with grief, went home because the next day was the Sabbath (Saturday) and no work could be done.

Early on Sunday morning, several women went to the tomb to anoint Jesus' body with spices and ointment and tend to it properly. But they were shocked when they discovered the stone had been rolled away from the entrance of the tomb. They were even more shocked to find an angel was sitting on the stone. "His appearance was like lightning, and his clothing white as snow" (Matt. 28:3). He spoke to the women:

Don't be afraid, for I know that you seek Jesus, who has been crucified. He is not here, for he has risen, just like he said. Come, see the place where the Lord was lying. Go quickly and tell his disciples, "He has risen from the dead, and behold, he goes before you into Galilee; there you will see him." Behold, I have told you (Matt. 28:5–7).

The women ran quickly from the tomb, both terrified and filled with joy. As they ran, they bumped into Jesus himself, who said, "Rejoice!" (Matt. 28:9). They fell at his feet and worshiped him. Then, Jesus told the women to leave him and go share their good news with Jesus' apostles and his other followers. "Tell them I will see them soon," Jesus said as the women ran toward the city.

The day that Jesus was crucified, it appeared that evil had won, that wicked men had been able to unjustly execute an innocent man and snuff out the voice of kindness, wisdom, and truth. But the empty tomb on Sunday morning proved that evil did *not* win. Jesus scored the ultimate victory of life over death, of good over evil. From that day on, death no longer represented the final ending but instead the glorious beginning: the gateway to God's Kingdom of Heaven.

Of course, the war between good and evil didn't end there but still plays out in our world and in our lives, each and every day. But Jesus' death and resurrection give us the power to conquer evil in our own lives if we are willing to get down on our knees, ask God for forgiveness for our sins, and commit our lives to following our Lord and Savior, Jesus Christ.

WHAT DO YOU THINK?

- When Jesus appeared before the women who had gone to his tomb, can you imagine what an amazing reunion that was? How would you describe the emotions they must have been feeling in that moment?

- How would the message of salvation be different if Jesus had died a natural death versus his death on the cross?

- Imagine if you lived in the time before Jesus came to earth. Describe how your view of death would have been different than it is today.

- How does the battle of good versus evil play out in your own life? What do you do to ensure that good wins out over evil?

Chapter 58

SERIOUSLY? ONE LITTLE COMMENT, AND I'LL NEVER BE JUST PLAIN OL' THOMAS AGAIN?

(JOHN 20:19–29)

Thomas needed proof. The other disciples kept saying they had seen Jesus. But Thomas was nobody's fool. He saw Jesus hanging on that cross and then watched them remove his lifeless body. People don't just "show up" after something like that. So Thomas wanted physical proof that Jesus had risen from the dead. And, for that, he will forever be remembered as "Doubting Thomas."

It all started one evening after Christ's burial when all of the apostles, except Thomas, were together. They were huddled in a room with all the doors locked, scared the Jewish leaders would be coming after them next. That's when Jesus appeared, right in the middle of the locked room, and gave the disciples his blessing. The next day, when the other disciples told Thomas what had happened, he stubbornly told them: "Unless I see in his hands the print of the nails, put my finger into the print of the nails, and put my hand into his side, I will not believe" (John 20:25).

Soon thereafter, the apostles were again together behind locked doors and Jesus appeared to them again. But this time, Thomas was with them. Jesus told Thomas to come over close to him. Thomas saw the holes in Jesus' hands from being nailed to the cross. Jesus then instructed Thomas: "Reach here your finger, and see my hands. Reach here your hand, and put it into my side" (John 20:27). Thomas declared, "My Lord and my God!" (John 20:28). Jesus then said to Thomas: "Because you have seen me, you have believed. Blessed are those who have not seen and have believed" (John 20:29).

Jesus didn't tell Thomas he was a horrible person for doubting or that, as a result, he would suffer some severe consequence. That's good news for all of us because, the fact is, just about everyone doubts at one time or another. Sometimes we question the very existence of God. Or our hope in the afterlife might falter. And sometimes we doubt whether Jesus truly is the human embodiment of God himself.

Our doubts often surface when our life gets off track and we stop praying, or when we engage in behaviors that we know will drive a wedge between us and the Lord. Other times, we doubt when we hear about a terrible tragedy, like the killing of an innocent child or the death of thousands of people in a natural disaster. Sometimes our doubts get the best of us for no good reason at all. We just feel that the very concept of God and the spiritual world isn't logical, like it all was just made up by someone with a really active imagination.

Even the most devout Christians have had their moments of doubt. A perfect example was Mother Teresa of Calcutta. In 1928, at the age of eighteen, she left the comfort of her home and family to become a Catholic nun and Christian missionary. She devoted her entire life to following Jesus by helping the poorest of the poor in the worst slums of India. She cared for the total outcasts; many were mentally ill or physically disabled or dying in the streets from starvation or disease.

One of the ways Mother Teresa showed her love for Jesus was to make sure that poor and abandoned people had a dignified death. She brought them in, fed them, and cleaned them up. She even cut their gnarly old toenails! Mother Teresa would sit by their bedside and hold their hands so that these poor souls would feel loved in their final days on earth.

By all accounts, this extraordinary woman prayed constantly and devoted her entire life to serving God. But even Mother Teresa had her moments of doubt. In 2007, many excerpts from Mother Teresa's own private journals were published in a book, *Come Be My Light*. In some of her writings, Mother Teresa cried out to God and expressed her inner torment, questioning her own faith and the very existence of God. She describes a period of spiritual darkness in which she felt the pain and emptiness of being unable to hear the voice of Jesus, as she had in her younger days. Still, she never turned her back on Jesus or God's calling for her truly remarkable life.

And that brings us to the second point of the story of Doubting Thomas. While Jesus did not tell Thomas that he would burn in hell for doubting his resurrection, he also didn't let Thomas off the hook entirely. He gave him a slap on the wrist by saying, in essence, "Okay, now that you have seen me with your own two eyes, you believe. But you kinda blew it, my friend. You should have believed without having to poke your germy fingers in the holes in my bright and shiny new spiritual body, especially given all that you witnessed while we were here on earth together."

So what does this mean for us? Does God want us to believe whatever anyone tells us about Jesus? Of course not. There are a lot of phonies in this world who will say just about anything, all in the name of God, in order to get what they want from us. Be on guard: being a Christian doesn't mean being a sucker. But that's not what was going on with Thomas, who had witnessed the many miracles that Jesus performed and even heard Christ foretell of his own death and resurrection (Matt. 17:22–23). Thomas really didn't have a good reason for doubting when his best friends told him about seeing Jesus.

To be sure, there will be periods in your own life when your faith will be shaken. But don't harden your heart and allow doubt to rule over you. Instead, remind yourself of all the times that God intervened when you needed him most, or those days you felt so close to him. Be honest with the Lord and lay your doubts at his feet, and he will help you overcome them. Then, you can expect to receive the blessings that God bestows upon his followers who believe, though they have not seen.

WHAT DO YOU THINK?

- Have you ever doubted the existence of God or that Jesus is our savior? What was going on in your life that may have triggered your doubts?
- Do you think people should be punished or rewarded depending on what they believe or don't believe? Is there some element of choice or accountability for what we believe?
- When our faith is weak, what actions can we take to help restore or strengthen it?

Chapter 59

DUDE, I THINK YOUR HAIR'S ON FIRE

(JOHN 21; ACTS 1–2)

Dear Diary,

It's only been about fifty days since Jesus was crucified, but it feels like a lifetime ago. And today was another unbelievable day, maybe the most over-the-top incredible day of my life, and I've had a LOT of those in the last three years. But I'm happy to report that I no longer feel like a "preacher-in-training." From here on in, I'll be leading the charge.

Before I get into what happened today, I gotta back up a bit. The night that I denied Jesus really shook me up. I know that God forgives us for even our worst sins, but I couldn't forgive myself. I had turned my back on the person I care about most in the world during his darkest hour, and I just couldn't get past it. Of course, I was overjoyed when he rose from the dead, but I also felt pretty weird around him too. I tried not to get too close to him—I didn't know what I would do if he brought up that night. But then he appeared to a few of us one morning after we had been out fishing. When we got back to shore, Jesus was sitting there, preparing our breakfast over a charcoal fire.

After we ate and chatted a bit, he turned to me directly. Looking straight into my eyes, he asked, "Do you love me?" I said, "Yes, Lord, you know I love you." And then he asked me the same question a second time, and then a third. At first, it made me feel bad, like he was doubting my love for him. But then I realized why he asked me this question three times: it was the same number of times I denied him that night after he was arrested.

It was like he was letting me undo the damage I had done, one denial at a time, and be restored to my place within God's plan and in Jesus' heart. Jesus then told me to feed and take care of his sheep and to follow him. I know that means he expects me to take care of his followers. With that, my torment was over. I was much more at peace with myself, and I was fully ready to take on whatever challenges were ahead of me. I just wasn't at all sure what those challenges would be.

The last time we saw Jesus was about a week and a half ago. Jesus told us to get back here to Jerusalem because God wanted us all together for the moment he was ready to baptize us "in the Holy Spirit" (Acts 1:1-4). We weren't exactly sure what that meant, but we knew it was going to be something big. We asked Jesus if he was about to free Israel from Roman rule, and he told us not to worry about such things. Instead, we should all be focused on our spiritual mission: being witnesses of Jesus throughout the world. And all of a sudden, Jesus started drifting away from us, floating upward. We watched him as he sailed up higher and higher and disappeared into the clouds. It was pretty amazing. But it was also sad. I somehow knew Jesus was ascending into heaven and that this would be the last time we'd see him here on earth, at least in bodily form. So we returned back to Jerusalem just like Jesus told us to do.

Now, as for today. We were all together with a big group of believers, including Jesus' mother, Mary, and his brothers. There were probably about 120 of us in all (see Acts 1:12-15, 2:1). We suddenly heard this loud sound of rushing air, like a strong wind blowing toward us. Then, I looked at the other disciples and noticed there was a flame, shaped like a tongue, sitting just above their heads. Sure enough, I had a flame hovering over me too.

When we started to talk about the flames, we realized that we were speaking in different languages, languages that we don't even know. While all this was going on, we felt the unmistakable feeling of God's spirit overtaking us. It was like we were transformed, right then and there, into more powerful versions of ourselves. I felt this intense energy, like I never experienced before. I could tell from looking at the people around me that they were feeling it too.

Of course, today is Pentecost, also called the Feast of Firstfruits, so Jerusalem is packed with people coming to give thanks to God for the grain and other food he provided during the harvest. There are Jewish people here from all over the world, many of whom speak foreign languages. I guess the rushing wind we heard inside the house could be heard outside too because thousands of people gathered to see what was happening. We headed out and started trying out our new languages.

The crowd was amazed because we were speaking in so many different tongues. Unfortunately, there are always a few haters in the crowd. Just because we were speaking languages that they didn't understand, they accused us of being drunk, like we were just a bunch of babbling idiots. That's when I decided I needed to get over my insecurities and start living up to the name Jesus gave me: Peter, the rock.

I hopped up on a table and raised my arms so everyone would be quiet. "How could we be drunk at nine in the morning?" I asked them. "We were talking in foreign languages because God had poured down his spirit on us, exactly how Jesus had predicted." Then I got really dramatic.

"People of Israel, listen to me! Jesus of Nazareth was a man of God who did many wonders and signs for you. And you turned him over to lawless men who killed him. But God raised him up because death could not hold him!" Then I showed them how King David had prophesied about Jesus and his resurrection.

To be honest, as I was preaching, I did have a moment of doubt. I heard that voice inside my head saying: "Hey, Simon: who do you think you are? Standing up here on this table and preaching like you're something special. Stop pretending that you're anything but a simple-minded fisherman." It was the same horrifying feeling I had when I was walking on the water and felt myself sinking. But I took a deep breath and looked above the crowd so I could picture Jesus' face. I looked into his eyes and my raging storm of doubt and fear was instantly silenced. I regained my courage and I yelled out: "Let all the house of Israel therefore know certainly that God has made him both Lord and Christ, this Jesus whom you crucified" (Acts 2:36).

And wow, did that get a reaction. Many people in the crowd started crying. Others just got very pale. And they started calling out to us, "Brothers, what shall we do?" (Acts 2:37).

I called back, "Repent, and be baptized, every one of you, in the name of Jesus Christ for the forgiveness of sins, and you will receive the gift of the Holy Spirit" (Acts 2:38). Surrender your lives to God, I told them, and stop devoting yourselves to selfish ambition, pride, greed, jealousy, and all of the other sins that get between us and our Creator. Unless you stay connected to God, I told the crowd, your lives will be filled with only hopelessness and despair.

Looking back on all this, I truly believe the Lord was speaking through me. Because after I was done preaching, around 3,000 people were baptized! They will now receive the gift of the Holy Spirit and share in the gift of salvation.

So, Diary, I have no more doubts. The rest of the disciples and I are ready to continue Jesus' work here on earth. And, with God's help, I'm sure we will overcome whatever challenges come our way. No more dress rehearsals. It's showtime!

In confidence and hope,

Peter

WHAT DO YOU THINK?

- Jesus asked three times if Peter truly loved him. Luke 10:27 states: "You shall love the Lord your God with all your heart, with all your soul, with all your strength, and with all your mind." Do you truly love the Lord? Is it even possible to love someone you have never met, at least in the physical sense? What does the word "love" even mean in this context?

- What do you think the apostles were feeling when God poured down his spirit and gave them the gift of speaking in tongues? What conflicting emotions do you think they might have experienced?

- How do you think the apostles reacted when thousands of people came to be baptized and devote their life to Jesus' teaching? Do you think they spent more time reflecting on the past few years with Jesus or on the road that was ahead of them?

Chapter 60

THE EVIL TENTMAKER TURNED SAINTLY

(ACTS 6–7; 8:1–8; 9:1–22)

When Jesus was crucified, the Jewish leaders believed they had eliminated both him and his message. They soon realized how wrong they were. Jesus' crucifixion wasn't the end—it was just the beginning. His ascension into heaven and the miracles of Pentecost only accelerated the spread of Jesus' teachings and the number of people who believed that his life, death, and resurrection had opened a new path to God. That good news, the Gospel of Jesus, was spreading faster than ever, so the Jewish leaders began aggressively persecuting anyone who was caught spreading it.

In chapter 29, you learned that Saint Stephen was one of the first martyrs of the Christian church, killed because he believed in the Gospel of Jesus. Stephen was a staunch follower of Jesus who served as a deacon in the early church, providing both financial and spiritual care for widows and others in need. He also was a vocal critic of the Jewish establishment for rejecting Jesus as the Messiah. So the Sanhedrin, the same body of religious leaders who had "convicted" Jesus of blasphemy, accused Stephen of the same crime and brought him in for a hearing.

Stephen launched into a speech describing how Jewish religious leaders had rejected God's messengers throughout history and Stephen accused the current leaders of being "betrayers and murderers" of the Son of God (Acts 7:51–53). The Jewish leaders became so enraged that they grabbed Stephen and carried him to the edge of the city, where they could stone him to death. To make sure their throwing arms wouldn't be restricted, they peeled off their outer coats and jackets and tossed them at the feet of a young Pharisee named Saul, so he could keep the clothes safe while they were brutally murdering Stephen.

Saul was glad to see Stephen die because he thought the followers of Jesus were threatening the Jewish faith. An educated man from a prominent Jewish family, Saul was originally from the city of Tarsus, a thriving trade center in what is now Turkey. He made his living as a tentmaker but made his reputation as a savage crusader against the early Christian leaders, beginning with those living in Jerusalem. He and his henchmen broke into their homes and dragged them off to prison.

As persecution increased in Jerusalem, the followers of Jesus fled to other regions, taking the Gospel with them. So Saul turned his attention there too. His plan was to start with Damascus, which is now the capital of Syria. He obtained permission from the Jewish leaders to travel to Damascus and arrest and torment any Christians he could find there and bring them back to Jerusalem.

"Breathing threats and slaughter against the disciples of the Lord" (Acts 9:1), Saul set off toward Damascus. But just before

Saul reached his destination, the Lord stopped him in his tracks. A light from the heavens surrounded Saul, knocking him to the ground and totally blinding him. As he lay helpless on the ground, Saul heard a voice from heaven.

"Saul, Saul, why do you persecute me?"

He said, "Who are you, Lord?"

The Lord said, "I am Jesus, whom you are persecuting. But rise up and enter into the city, then you will be told what you must do."
(Acts 9:4–6)

The men traveling with Saul had seen the light and heard a sound but couldn't figure out what had just happened. All they knew for sure was that Saul was completely blind, so they had to carefully guide him into Damascus. For his first three days in the city, Saul prayed and fasted, not eating or drinking a thing.

While Saul was praying, the Lord spoke in a vision to a follower of Jesus named Ananias, who lived in Damascus. The Lord told Ananias to go to Saul, lay his hands on him, and give him a blessing. Ananias expressed serious reservations about this plan. "Lord, I have heard from many about this man, how much evil he did to your saints at Jerusalem. Here he has authority from the chief priests to bind all who call on your name" (Acts 9:13–14).

But the Lord assured Ananias he had nothing to worry about. In fact, he said Saul was about to become Jesus' most loyal supporter. "He is my chosen vessel to bear my name before the nations and kings, and the children of Israel" to spread the good news that Jesus brought to the world (Acts 9:15).

So Ananias went to Saul and blessed him. In that moment, Saul became filled with the Holy Spirit and "something like scales fell from his eyes." Saul regained his sight, was baptized, and started proclaiming that Jesus is the son of God in the city's synagogues (Acts 9:17–20). God transformed Saul from a tyrant dedicated to persecuting Christians to his most devoted and passionate soldier in the fight to save souls and establish the new Christian church. Later, Saul started using the name "Paul," the Greek version of his name, to help him connect with people who were gentiles—not Jewish—as he preached to them.

From the time of Paul's conversion until the time of his death, he traveled thousands of miles throughout what is now Europe and the Middle East, establishing Christian churches and teaching Jesus' message of salvation. Because of his devotion to the Gospel, Paul was persecuted, jailed, beaten, ridiculed, and tormented by both Roman authorities and the Jewish establishment, of which he once was a prominent member. Paul will forever be credited with doing more than anyone, apart from Jesus himself, to establish what we now know as Christianity. Much of our fundamental Christian doctrine and understanding of how followers of Jesus should live come from Paul's letters to the early Christian churches. At least thirteen of the books of the New Testament were written by Paul, starting with Romans and ending with Philemon.

Paul's immense contribution to Christianity makes his life's story the ultimate lesson on redemption. He started out as one of the bad guys. There was no limit to how far he would go to punish anyone he perceived as a threat to the Jewish laws, customs, and traditions. But the Lord chose to use Paul's strength, passion, intelligence, and commitment for his own purposes. When Jesus himself called out to Paul on the road to Damascus, Paul's heart was transformed. He surrendered himself to the Lord and devoted the rest of his life to spreading the Holy Gospel.

God makes the gift of redemption available to each and every one of us. When the Lord calls you—and he will—you have to decide whether to ignore him and dig even deeper into your life of sin, emptiness, and ultimately death. Or answer the call and let God change your heart. If you choose to listen to God, he will remove the scales from your eyes so you can see the truth and the Lord in his full glory. That is when your journey on the path to eternal joy and salvation will truly begin.

WHAT DO YOU THINK?

- Paul was well-known for his brutal persecution of Christians. So why would God choose him to play a key role in establishing the early Christian church?
- Does it surprise you that a man who once was so committed to destroying the early Christians and snuffing out Jesus' message could then become even more passionate and devoted to preaching the Gospel of Jesus and converting people to Christianity?
- Do you think surrendering yourself to Jesus and bringing him into your heart requires a specific moment of conversion or can it happen over a period of time?

Chapter 61

REVELATION: THE ZOMBIE APOCALYPSE ON STEROIDS

(REVELATION 1–22)

If you're into science fiction, especially apocalyptic, epic nail-biters about foreboding mythical creatures battling it out to the death, you'll probably like the book of Revelation. This final book of the New Testament was written as a letter to the seven early churches in Asia but mainly includes religious prophecy. It is a God-inspired vision describing spiritual battles that have played out since the beginning of time and predicts how it all will come to an end in the world's final days.

While some biblical scholars disagree on the book's author, who identifies himself only as John, there is a consensus that it was written in the first century after the birth of Christ on the Greek island of Patmos. Revelation delivers one powerful punch as a strange, action-packed, futuristic thriller. Here are the highlights.

God was sitting on his throne in heaven, surrounded by twenty-four elders and four six-winged creatures covered in eyeballs. A lamb, representing Jesus, with seven horns and seven eyes took from God a book bound shut with seven seals. One by one, the lamb broke the seals, bringing forth a different vision with each. First, four horses appeared, each with a rider on a mission, like fighting wars, eliminating peace from earth, establishing society's commercial system, and bringing death into the world. The breaking of the other seals set in motion a bunch of natural disasters and cosmic turmoil, like a star falling to earth; parts of the sun, moon, and stars growing dark; a horrible earthquake; and violent thunder and lightning.

The main villain was a red, seven-headed dragon with ten horns and seven crowns. The dragon represented none other than the Devil himself, who waged war on heaven and earth with the help of two beasts, to which the dragon gave full power and authority. The first beast resembled a leopard but with the feet of a bear and the mouth of a lion. This beast was the embodiment of the Antichrist, speaking against God and Jesus, doing everything it could to turn people against the Lord. The second beast resembled a lamb, and it performed miraculous signs to trick people into worshiping the Antichrist beast. This "lamb" beast, whose number was 666, required every person to bear its mark on either their right hand or forehead, indicating their pledge of loyalty to it. Those who refused to bear the mark of the beast would suffer the consequences, which meant being cast out from the world's commercial system so that they couldn't buy food or anything else needed to survive.

Although the Devil's battalion of evildoers did everything in their power to vanquish the Lord and his followers, the good guys prevailed in the end. God's army, led by a soldier riding on a white horse, battled and overcame the two beasts, which "were thrown alive into the lake of fire that burns with sulfur" (Rev. 19:20). The dragon was imprisoned in an abyss for 1,000 years and then released to Earth, where he attempted to trick people into following him and his evil ways. But he was ultimately defeated when he and his supporters waged a final war on the people of God in which the bad guys were overtaken by fire. The dragon was thrown alive into the lake of fire to join the two beasts, where they "will be tormented day and night forever and ever" (Rev. 20:10).

In the end, everyone who ever lived was brought before God for the final judgment. At that time, the "Book of Life" was read, which contained the names of the people who lived on earth, along with whatever good or bad acts each committed. Anyone whose name was not listed in the Book of Life was thrown into the lake of fire. And a new heaven and a new world emerged where there would be no more death or suffering.

It would be easy to dismiss the book of Revelation as the end-of-world rantings of one man with an active imagination. However, its placement as the very last book of the Bible highlights its significance as a vital piece of spiritual prophecy with a critically important message. Through the use of religious symbolism and apocalyptic imagery, Revelation gives us a peek behind the curtain at the battle between good and evil that has existed since the creation of our universe and will continue until the world ends on the day of God's final judgment.

In the visible world that surrounds us, true evil doesn't take the form of multiheaded dragons or ferocious creatures with mystical powers. If it did, then the Devil likely would attract far fewer souls. Instead, the real soldiers in Satan's army often are successful, well-dressed, and well-spoken social, cultural, or political influencers. They might even be our next-door neighbors who appear to be nice, fun people, but who profess a view, whether subtly or directly, that God doesn't exist or at least isn't relevant.

These people reject Jesus' message that the way to achieve real joy and eternal life is to surrender yourself to God and serve one another with humility, kindness, and love. They degrade our world and our very humanity when they remove our Lord from the equation and advance a value system centered on pride, self-indulgence, unhealthy competition, and contempt for anyone who puts God at the center of their lives.

But the battle between good and evil that poses the greatest threat to our lives, our futures, and our very souls isn't the one happening in the world around us. It is being fought every day inside our own minds and hearts. And the outcome most certainly will determine our fate.

The book of Revelation teaches us that in Jesus' final coming, the curse of evil will be lifted, and there will be no darkness or nighttime, only God's beautiful light. In the end, we all will be brought before the Lord for the final judgment, according to Revelation 22:12–15. Those who have committed their lives to serving the Lord will enter his kingdom and see his glorious face, as he sits on his throne with Jesus at his side (Rev. 22:3–5).

Let's be honest: life can be incredibly hard. At times, it is filled with much pain, frustration, and sadness. And we all have periods in our lives when our faith is weak, we stumble and fall, and we give in to temptation. But although no one is perfect, we all have a choice to make. We can choose the path of those who oppose God and reject his gift of eternal salvation. If we do, we will forever be shackled with the spirit-crushing weight of sin and will find ourselves, again and again, back in a place filled only with emptiness and despair.

Or we can choose to follow Jesus and commit ourselves to living according to his teachings. Only then will we live joyfully in God's brilliant light with true meaning and purpose. And if we do ask God into our hearts, our journeys here on earth will end in his magnificent kingdom, where we will live in peace with our Heavenly Father and our Lord Jesus Christ forever and ever.

Only you can choose which path you will take, and how the story of your own life will be written.

WHAT DO YOU THINK?

- Why do you think God created the world so that good and evil aren't nearly as obvious as they are in the book of Revelation? Why are the battles, and often the bad guys, cloaked in less visible and subtler forms?
- Provide a specific example of where you see the battle between good and evil in the world around us? How about inside of you?
- Have you committed your life to God? If not, what is stopping you?

ABOUT THE AUTHOR

Spencer C. Demetros is a dad and lifelong student of Scripture. By trade, he is a business attorney in the technology industry. But in recent years, he answered God's call to use his no-nonsense but loving parental instincts, combined with his unique storytelling ability and irreverent brand of humor, to deliver God's Word in an entertaining and relatable way to young readers, wherever they are in their journeys with Christ. Spencer lives in the small New England town of Harvard, Massachusetts, with his wife, Catherine, and teenage twins. Visit him online at www.spencerdemetros.com.